D0497966

# Free Agents

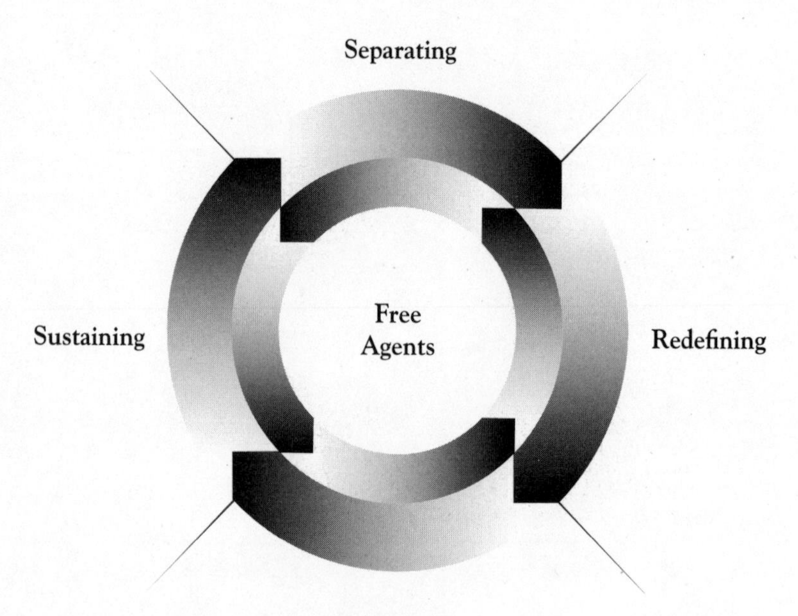
Separating
Free
Agents
Sustaining
Redefining
Positioning

# Free Agents

**People and Organizations Creating a New Working Community**

Susan B. Gould

Kerry J. Weiner

Barbara R. Levin

Jossey-Bass Publishers • San Francisco

Substantial discounts on bulk quantities of Jossey-Bass books are available to corporations, professional associations, and other organizations. For details and discount information, contact the special sales department at Jossey-Bass Inc., Publishers (415) 433–1740; Fax (800) 605–2665.

For sales outside the United States, please contact your local Simon & Schuster International Office.

Jossey-Bass Web address: http://www.josseybass.com

Manufactured in the United States of America on Lyons Falls Pathfinder Tradebook. This paper is acid-free and 100 percent totally chlorine-free.

**Library of Congress Cataloging-in-Publication Data**

Gould, Susan B., 1937-
Free agents : people and organizations creating a new working community / Susan B. Gould, Kerry J. Weiner, Barbara R. Levin. — 1st ed.
p. cm. — (The Jossey-Bass business & management series)
Includes bibliographical references and index.
ISBN 0-7879-0283-7 (acid-free paper)
1. Employee empowerment. 2. Management. 3. Work groups. 4. Organizational behavior. I. Weiner, Kerry J., 1952- . II. Levin, Barbara R., 1933- . III. Title. IV. Series.
HD50.5.G68 1997
650.1—dc21 96-45859

Credits are on page 185.

FIRST EDITION
*HB Printing* 10 9 8 7 6 5 4 3 2 1

The Jossey-Bass

Business & Management Series

# Contents

Preface xv

Acknowledgments xxv

The Authors xxvii

1. Responding to Change 1
    - What Has Changed?
    - The Pain of Change
    - Embracing Change
    - Free Agent Code
    - Corporate Challenge
    - The New Ethic

**Part One: Becoming a Free Agent**

2. The Free Agent Process: Creating a New Future 19
    - Becoming a Free Agent
    - Feelings
    - Getting Started
    - Challenges
    - Am I There Yet?
    - Summing Up

3. Separating: Drawing the Final Curtain 31
    - Endings
    - Painful Feelings and Self-Defeating Behavior
    - Skills
    - Strategies
    - Moving On

4. Redefining: Moving Beyond Comfort 49
Obstacles
Strategies
Assembling Your Portfolio of Assets
Final Synthesis

5. Positioning: Staking Your Claim 63
Markets
Stresses and Strains
Skills
Strategies
Making Your Decision
Making the Sale

**Part Two: Becoming a Free Agent Community**

6. The Need for Corporate Change: Sailing into Uncharted Waters 85
The New Community
The Process of Building Community
Challenges
Accepting the Challenge

7. Corporate Separating: Embracing the New 95
Getting on Board
Clarity of Purpose
Communication
Control
Creating an Oasis

8. Redefining the Corporate Infrastructure 111
Communication Systems
Performance-Management Systems
Compensation Systems
Reward and Recognition Systems

9. Corporate Positioning 125

Matching Skills to Corporate Needs
Updating Recruiting and Hiring Systems
Providing Development Opportunities
Making It Easy for People to Leave
The Benefits

**Part Three: Sustaining Free Agents and a Free Agent Community**

10. Living the Free Agent Life 139

Why Commit to Being a Free Agent for Life?
The Free Agent Life
Feelings
Challenges
Strategies
Are You a Committed Free Agent?

11. Maintaining a Free Agent Community 153

The Sustaining Process
Sustaining a Dispersed Community

12. Free Agent Communities in Action 165

Entertainment Model
Publishing Model
High-Tech Model

References 175

For Further Information 179

Index 181

# Free Agents

*We dedicate this book to our clients with appreciation.*

# Preface

> The world of work is changing rapidly in a way that forces all of us to change. I thought I did not have anything to worry about, but I was wrong. The changes took me by surprise, and I had to transform my outlook. The process of becoming a Free Agent helped me get back on track and successfully chart my way in a whole new world.

Hal did everything "right"—attended the "best" schools, earned his degree, and entered the fast track. He is tough, knowledgeable, competent, driven, and loyal—an individual contributor and a good team player. But here he is with a pink slip in one hand, the door slammed behind him. He feels numb and alone. What went wrong? How can this be happening?

Sharon sits at her desk with her head in her hands. She has just lost three valuable contributors to her team—even Hal—as the result of "right sizing." How is she ever going to re-create the outstanding team and community she just destroyed? If she cannot offer job security to the people she has nurtured and mentored, what can she offer? She wonders whether she is cut out for the new roles she and other managers throughout the company are now being expected to play. Even if her job is not in jeopardy, can she commit herself to the company's shift in values? She seriously questions whether she still belongs in the organization.

The world of work has changed forever. Regardless of the industry, corporations are confronted with the challenge of changing the way they do business. As companies radically reconstruct themselves by streamlining their operations, people are living in constant fear of losing their jobs and their quality of life. They are frightened and distressed (Uchitelle, 1994, p. D1).

Talented and highly skilled individuals are finding that their careers are falling off track. Their lives are altered forever. Wave after wave of restructuring has washed away the promises of lifelong employment that had sustained their confidence in their future (Richman, 1995, p. 160). People are discovering that it is no longer a question of whether they will have a second or third career, but a question of when.

Since the mid-1980s our management consulting firm has been assisting individuals caught in this maelstrom. Our clients are either voluntarily or involuntarily reassessing their value in the marketplace and their relationship to their work. Over time they have come to recognize a new reality and are beginning to follow a new model, one in which they are in charge of their careers, their lives, and their future. They are becoming Free Agents in the world of business. As Free Agents, they define themselves by what they do rather than for whom they do it. They understand and accept that the relationship between themselves and their employers has shifted from "'til death do us part" to "What have you done for me lately?" (Stewart, 1995, p. 76). This realization provides Free Agents with a new psychological freedom. They have successfully replaced the idea of employment security with employability, and they understand that they alone are responsible for acquiring the skills they need to find work (Filipczak, 1995, p. 30). By being dependent on themselves alone, they are able to develop a new kind of security (Noble, 1995a, p. 23).

From our research and professional experience, we have become convinced that individuals no longer have a choice of whether to become Free Agents. The Free Agent model is not new. It prevailed prior to the Industrial Revolution and pervades modern-day sports. Today it is becoming increasingly clear that to survive in business you need to depend on your own skills and expertise for your identity and security rather than on a company. Those who cannot make the change will be left out.

As we observed Free Agents in the marketplace, we noticed that they are often catalysts for corporate change. With intensified competition, rising customer expectations, and demands for faster product development, companies increasingly require the skills, creativity, and flexibility that Free Agents provide. As more people become Free Agents, they create new needs and expectations in the workplace. They are aware of their value in the marketplace and have become increasingly discriminating about where they bring their skills. Companies are realizing that in order to meet Free Agents' expectations, they must change the way they run their businesses, manage their human resources, and define their relationship with the workforce. Once they provide an environment where Free Agents want to come and work, they will be able to attract a "highly productive, creative, empowered, quality workforce" (Filipczak, 1995, p. 30).

We have interviewed individuals within companies to discover how they are meeting these challenges. And we have spent the better part of our professional lives as Free Agents ourselves. *Free Agents* is the result of our findings as well as of our personal experiences. We have written this book as a resource for individuals and corporations trying to define new roles and relationships, reestablish balance, and create a new workplace community. For the individual we provide a process that we have developed and used with hundreds of clients. We include many real-life examples and describe the feelings of real people who have gone through this process. The strategies we present work; we have seen them in action. In our interviews and reading we discovered that companies go through the same process when they attempt to align Free Agents' needs with their need to create a community of common purpose. Although many corporations are groping for the answers to the questions we raise in this book, there are few definitive solutions. We provide some ideas that we hope will spur organizations on in their attempts to create a Free Agent community.

## Who Should Read This Book?

Whether you are currently working or are searching for work, you will find *Free Agents* compelling. The term "Free Agent" usually refers to an individual working outside an organization. In this book, though, Free Agents are everyone in the workplace. Senior executives, managers, human resource professionals, individual employees, and freelancers, contractors, and consultants will find the material in this book relevant.

### *Senior Executives*

This book shows you how to improve the competitive advantage of your company by creating and sustaining a Free Agent community. It provides you, as the architect of change, with a process for systematically building a community where flexible, skilled professionals will want to work. It helps you think strategically about vision as the driver of your company's culture, values, and operations.

### *Managers*

As a manager in an organization, you play a critical role in initiating change and creating a Free Agent community. Be aware that you may face two major challenges. The first is making the commitment to becoming a Free Agent yourself. You will have to deal with your own feelings and emotions about the changing rules in the workplace and about your career. If you are not prepared to become a Free Agent yourself, it will be difficult to build and manage a Free Agent team.

The second major challenge for you is to provide leadership in developing an infrastructure for your Free Agent community. Your company's hiring, communication, performance-management, and compensation systems need to support an environment in which Free Agents can produce their best results.

This book provides you with a step-by-step process for becoming a Free Agent yourself, helping others on your team to become Free Agents, and building a Free Agent community of common purpose.

### *Human Resource Professionals*

As a human resource professional, you can be extremely influential in assisting managers assume the new roles that are required of them, in helping individuals adopt and sustain a Free Agent mentality, and in redesigning and implementing the systems that are needed to create and preserve a Free Agent community.

*Free Agents* provides you with a process for helping people in your organization become and remain Free Agents. You can give this book to individuals at all levels to help them begin thinking and acting as Free Agents. You can also use this book as a resource for overhauling your organization's infrastructure to meet Free Agents' needs. You will see how other companies and teams are rebuilding their systems to develop a community of common purpose, and you can then use the information in this book to reconfigure your organization.

### *Individual Employees*

Although you currently have a position in an organization, in order to justify that position you must demonstrate your value to the company on a daily basis. As a professional or knowledge worker, freeing yourself from an unhealthy dependence on the corporation and feeling, thinking, and acting like a Free Agent increase your value to your organization and in the marketplace. This book guides you through the process of becoming a Free Agent; it shows you how to redefine your relationship to your employer and your work.

### *Freelancers, Contractors, Consultants*

Individuals who are self-employed contend with discontinuity and uncertainty in their work situations. *Free Agents* provides skills and tactics for coping with the anxieties that are endemic in the Free Agent life. It offers suggestions for expanding your ideas about a career, work opportunities, and employability.

*Free Agents* shows how to gain control in a rapidly changing world. It provides a formula for assuming increased autonomy and independence. It describes a process for redesigning your career and reframing your relationship with your work and your workplace. Regardless of your position, this book shows you how other people have successfully started new work lives as Free Agents, have dealt with the fears and risks of being Free Agents, and have become Free Agents for life. Like them, you too will become the catalyst for changing your workplace. All you need to add is commitment, perseverance, and energy, and you will be on your way to creating a Free Agent community.

## How We Wrote This Book

As Free Agents ourselves, we are involved in a process of lifelong learning. Over the past ten years we have personally observed and assisted over a thousand professionals experiencing the process and coping with the challenges of becoming and remaining Free Agents as they strive to succeed in a new work world. These individuals became our laboratory. In our one-on-one client sessions and our bimonthly group meetings we watched these professionals wrestle with their bewilderment about having to change, their fright and pain, their difficulty getting beyond job titles, their confusion about how to market themselves, and their struggles to find a workplace that captured their enthusiasm and commitment.

Together with our clients we refined a process for helping them through this tough time, and we developed strategies, some more successful than others, for reshaping their lives. Observing how our clients coped, rethought who they were, decided what to do next, and maintained their momentum further informed the process over the years. This book grew out of our clients' enthusiasm for the process and their eagerness to share their experiences in becoming Free Agents in the hope of helping others. We based our original ideas on observations and informal interviews. We then followed up with extensive reading and formal interviews.

We built an enthusiastic referral network throughout the country as we conducted over fifty structured interviews with senior executives, managers, and professionals who were self-employed or employed in one of thirty-nine companies. These organizations ranged from Fortune 500 companies to entrepreneurial start-ups in many different industries. The interviews lasted from one to two hours and were conducted face-to-face and by telephone. In the interviews, we posed a series of open-ended questions that probed for facts and feelings. How would you describe yourself and your work situation? What made you decide to become a Free Agent? When and how did you know you were a Free Agent? What do you worry about at two o'clock in the morning? We also questioned the ways corporate leaders and managers run their companies and manage their people—especially their Free Agent workforce. We heard about managers who were using anachronistic methods and others who had adopted liberating new ways of managing people. We got a consistent picture of the new relationship being forged between Free Agents and their employers.

The stories we heard were different in each case; yet as the people we were interviewing described their experiences, similar themes emerged. *Free Agents* is their book and contains their stories. The process presented in this book blends our experience, our readings, and all the stories we heard. It provides a framework for individuals attempting to drive their careers and build a workplace community. The otherwise unattributed quotes that begin chapters and sections are candid comments made by those we interviewed and by our clients. The people whose stories we tell throughout the book are composites of real individuals.

## How Is the Book Organized?

After the first chapter, which outlines the reasons why individuals and businesses need to change, *Free Agents* is divided into three parts. Part One, "Becoming a Free Agent," focuses on the process individuals go through in reframing their relationship with the marketplace and their work. Chapter Two describes a process that both those who are employed and those who are not can follow in order to become Free Agents. The remaining chapters in this part guide readers through the steps in this process. We discuss the pain of discarding old beliefs and separating from a job, colleagues, a company, and a community. We also share strategies that individuals can use for listing and analyzing their assets and assessing their value in the marketplace. Finally we describe how individuals who have identified their marketable skills can position themselves in new markets.

Part Two, "Becoming a Free Agent Community," describes in detail the organization's responsibility for creating an environment in which Free Agents can do their best work. In this part, we explain a process that companies can use to reclaim a vital and dynamic workforce. We discuss the importance of revitalizing the corporate vision as a way of creating a community of purpose. We look at ways of making the vision operational, and we also examine how companies must position themselves in the marketplace to attract the skilled employees they need for success.

Part Three, "Sustaining Free Agents and a Free Agent Community," identifies the issues facing individuals and organizations in maintaining a Free Agent life and a Free Agent community. We provide strategies for both. At the end of the book we describe three industries that exemplify Free Agent communities in various stages of development.

*Free Agents* is a response to the pain and confusion that have permeated corporate America. It is distilled from years of observation and from interviews with clients and nonclients. We hope you will use the book to transform yourself and transform your workplace.

November 1996

Susan B. Gould
Palo Alto, CA

Kerry J. Weiner
San Francisco, CA

Barbara R. Levin
Palo Alto, CA

# Acknowledgments

We would like to thank all our clients and everyone whom we interviewed for their contributions to this book. Their courage, persistence, and willingness to consider change make them models for all Free Agents. Without their openness, enthusiasm, and constant prodding this material would never have come to life.

We offer special thanks to all those colleagues and friends who took an interest in this project by reading, critiquing, keeping us on track, and supporting us when things seemed overwhelming. They probably did not realize how important their words of encouragement were to the project.

Bobbi Mark has our deepest appreciation. Her enthusiasm for our book and her guidance in helping us navigate the publishing world gave us direction and confidence.

To William Hicks at Jossey-Bass we owe gratitude for recognizing the value of our ideas and helping us to see broader applications. He, along with Cedric Crocker and Larry Alexander, provided the direction, focus, and editorial feedback critical to this book. A special thanks to Judith Hibbard for guiding us and the project along so smoothly, and to Pamela Fischer for her superb editing. Our sincere appreciation also to Lorie Meeks for her contribution to the production of this book.

The beauty and tranquillity of the northern California coast provided the perfect atmosphere for our creative efforts. Our writers' camp will forever hold a special place in our thoughts.

Most of all, we would like to thank our families for their flexibility and willingness to live without us for long periods. Their unselfishness enabled us to transform our percolating ideas into a cohesive message. Their love gave us the strength we needed to see this project through to completion.

# The Authors

**Susan B. Gould,** founder and president of Gould and Associates, a human resources consulting firm based in Palo Alto, California, has over twenty years of experience in executive coaching, performance coaching, team building, and career consulting in the private, nonprofit, and public sectors. Prior to founding Gould and Associates in 1988, she was director of the Public Management Program at Stanford University's Graduate School of Business. She was also secretary and treasurer of MJB Company, and director of administration and development for the San Francisco Conservatory of Music. She earned a B.A. degree from Connecticut College, an M.A. degree from Tufts University, and an M.B.A. degree from the Graduate School of Business at Stanford University. She currently sits on a number of boards of directors, including those of publicly traded and privately held companies as well as nonprofits.

**Kerry J. Weiner** is founder and president of Weiner Associates, a San Francisco-based human resources consulting firm. She has over fourteen years of experience in organizational development, performance management, training, and career consulting in Fortune 500 companies nationwide. She began her career as a writer and instructional designer developing training programs for the United States Army. She held a number of human resource management positions at Pacific Telephone and Levi Strauss prior to starting her own consulting business in 1984. She earned a B.A. degree from the State University of New York at Binghamton and an M.A.

degree in education from San Francisco State University. She has served on boards of directors for nonprofit organizations and is currently a director for an independent school in San Francisco.

**Barbara R. Levin** has more than twenty years of experience in career and organizational development, team building, and executive coaching through her work in psychology and the nonprofit sector. A human resources consultant with Gould and Associates, she specializes in assisting organizations and individuals who are undergoing transitions because of layoffs, restructuring, growth, or the rebalancing of workloads. Previously she was the executive director of EdSource, a California education-information agency. She began her career as a school psychologist with the San Mateo County Office of Education and the San Francisco Unified School District. She served as commissioner and vice chair of the Educational Management and Evaluation Commission of the California Department of Education. She earned a B.A. degree from Jackson College, Tufts University, and an M.A. degree from San Francisco State University.

*Chapter One*

# Responding to Change

> The most visible differences between the corporation of the future and its present-day counterpart will be not the products they make or the equipment they use—but who will be working, how they will be working, why they will be working, and what work will mean to them.
>
> —*R. Haas, "The Corporation Without Boundaries"*

As the door to his office closes, a smile spreads across Wade's face. He feels good about his decision. He is sure that Kathryn is the right choice. She is smart, experienced, and capable. She has solid credentials and an impressive track record. Beyond that, there is something different about her. Perhaps it is her belief in her skills and abilities. In the interview, she used her past accomplishments to demonstrate how her current skills would help the company meet its goals.

Although this industry is new to her, she had done her homework and had a grasp of the big picture. From her research she knew that the industry was expanding rapidly, and she was familiar with the key players. She had targeted this company because of its leadership position in the market. During the interviews, she asked good questions. She wanted to know the company's competitive strategy in the marketplace, Wade's vision for the company, and its ability to finance future growth. In addition, she asked about opportunities to acquire new skills. She was eager to find work that would enhance her abilities and allow her to keep learning. Throughout the multiple interviews, she exhibited a great deal of self-confidence. Everyone on the team was impressed with her analytic approach and her openness. They felt that she would fit into the company's culture.

Wade appreciated Katherine's self-reliant attitude. She was not surprised when he explained that the project might last only a year. She assumed that continued employment depended on her ability to keep her skills updated and to continually look for new opportunities within the company. She understood that when she could no longer provide value to the company, it would be time to leave. No doubt about it. Kathryn has the attitude that Wade wants on his team and the skills the company needs. Wade is pleased with his decision.

As the elevator doors shut, Kathryn breathes a deep sigh of relief. She cannot believe that the CEO just offered her an exciting opportunity as the project manager of the company's newest product line. She will be stepping into a management position that will allow her to change industries and leverage her current skills while learning new ones. All her work over the past ten months has paid off. The many hours researching new industries and the endless networking have brought her to this point.

Everything she heard about this company seems to be true. The people here are trying to create a collegial environment where individuals can produce their best work. This seems to be a community of individuals like herself who take responsibility for their work and will do whatever needs to be done to get results. She is delighted at the prospect of working with independence and autonomy. In her last position the company's tight controls often made her feel powerless to do her job effectively.

Kathryn is particularly impressed with the clarity of the company's vision. All employees understand how their performance contributes to profitability and how their projects fit with the corporate goals. The compensation package encourages and rewards both individual and team results. Kathryn is sure she is going to like it here—even if the job lasts only a short time. She is determined to contribute to the success of the company and learn as much as possible. This is where she belongs now. She is pleased with her decision.

Kathryn, Wade, and his company are composites of real people and organizations that are transforming the workplace by redefining the traditional relationship between employer and employee. Kathryn represents a breed of new workers—Free Agents—who possess the skills, attitude, and flexibility that companies need to remain viable as they face ever-increasing competition. Free Agents are those managers and professionals who recognize and accept an emerging redefinition of employment. Shedding timeworn ideas about long-term employment, they understand that the old paternalistic relationship between corporations and their employees no longer exists and that they are only as valuable as the sum of their skills (Ramirez, 1995, p. C11). Like Kathryn, they know that they must take the responsibility for finding interesting and rewarding work and for regularly acquiring new skills that will make them increasingly valuable in the marketplace.

To stay on the cutting edge, companies like Wade's are committed to attracting and retaining a skilled and flexible workforce. In their efforts to find and motivate such workers, they are discovering that Free Agents have needs that cannot be met by old systems and management practices. Companies are realizing that they have to make systemic changes to create environments where individuals like Kathryn will want to work and will be able to contribute to the bottom line.

Kathryn and Wade are part of the changing workplace. The new employee/employer relationship is based on the exchange of skills, increased productivity, and some degree of commitment to company purpose in return for opportunities to work on stimulating and challenging projects and to be part of a new kind of community (Waterman, Waterman, and Collard, 1994, p. 88). In such a community, corporate needs are met by acquiring and developing resourceful and flexible individuals who are capable of handling change and volatility. Individuals' needs are met because they are obtaining the additional skills and experience that will increase their future employability. In such a community, stability, predictability, and long-term employment are replaced with shared goals, mutual interdependence, and voluntary commitment. Those who succeed in this new community understand that their skills and ability to provide value in the marketplace provide the only path to employability.

## What Has Changed?

During the years following World War II, Americans believed that they had "almost a divine right to a very particular American dream entailing a home, a secure job, and a raise every year" (Uchitelle and Kleinfield, 1996, p. A14). An unwritten employer-employee contract became the norm. In this implied agreement, employees traded loyalty and devotion to a company for job security and other entitlements. Longevity was celebrated and valued (Markels and Lublin, 1995, p. B1). Employees were expected to remain with one company for their entire career and to "put their duty to the job ahead of almost everything else in life" (Noble, 1995b, p. B21).

There is no job security any longer. Thousands of people who never before had to worry about their jobs have been caught in the cross fire of corporate restructuring, downsizing, and layoffs. Over 2.2 million Americans lost their jobs from 1990 to 1995, about twice as many as lost jobs in the previous five years (Serwer, 1995, p. 14). According to a 1996 *New York Times* poll, almost three-quarters of all households have had a brush with layoffs since 1980. In one-third of all households a member of the family has lost a job, and nearly 40 percent more are aware of a relative, friend, or neighbor who was laid off. For the first time the educated, middle-aged, and well-paid segment of society has been hardest hit. Increasingly, the jobs that are disappearing are those of "higher-paid, white-collar workers, many at large corporations, women as well as men, many at the peak of their careers" (Uchitelle and Kleinfield, 1996,

p. A1). These individuals often experience a long and painful transition as they look for work in this turbulent work world.

Perhaps the most significant aspect of today's dislocation is the death of the unwritten contract. A veteran employee at a large company told this story about the mass layoff that took place in her group:

> As I drove up that morning, I saw the helicopter on the pad and I knew something awful was going to happen. The only time the executives came in by air was when they wanted to leave in a hurry. Otherwise, they took the two-hour limo ride. We were told to report to the cafeteria where they informed us that we were terminated. No warning, no praise for our work, no sign of gratitude for our contribution to the company. I had been there twelve years, a relative newcomer. There were others with much longer service. It was absolutely humiliating. You work so hard, and still you are gone tomorrow.

The media assured us that downsizing would end when the economic recovery began. But even with record profits companies continue to let employees go. Procter & Gamble's position is shared by many of the large corporations that account for the largest number of layoffs. "We must slim down to stay competitive. The consumer wants better value. Our competitors are getting leaner and quicker, and we are simply going to have to run faster to stay ahead" (Murray, 1995, p. A1).

While old jobs disappear, new ones are created. But the replacement work is different. Often the new positions are based on technology that requires new skills. The workplace is different too: as some sectors shrink, others expand (Cassidy, 1996, p. 55). Companies are finding out that cutting people will not in itself improve productivity, shareholders' return on investment, customer satisfaction, or product quality. Nor will it spark innovation or speed up decision making (Boyett and Boyett, 1995, p. 56). The answers seem to be embedded in more lasting and profound changes, in the ways in which companies and their work are organized, in "changes in the basic processes and behaviors by which a company operates" (Boyett and Boyett, 1995, p. 56). Companies now value creativity, agility, risk taking, and a high level of competence, not long-term loyalty. These are exactly the qualities that Free Agents possess. It is no longer a choice; even if all layoffs were to end tomorrow, individuals would still need to become Free Agents.

Few people, if any, can escape the effects of today's fast-paced economic change. In this new world, no one's job is safe; people are employed only as long as they add value to a company. Because corporations no longer take care of their employees for life, individuals themselves are responsible for discovering ways to increase their value. Free Agents like Kathryn realize these realities and are successful in this new work world.

## The Pain of Change

In a workplace where old certainties no longer apply, individuals are feeling an extremely high level of insecurity: "anxiety stalks the corridors" (Uchitelle and Kleinfield, 1996, p. A1). The end of the unwritten contract has created a huge void. Job apprehension is everywhere. As one client explains, "Although we should be happy to still have our jobs, all of us who are left are feeling outraged and scared. There seems to be a great deal of confusion about where our loyalties should lie. Many of us had to let our friends go. We could be next."

Many are not ready, or willing, to accept the demise of the implied contract and the end of predictability. They still wish for the old bond and are not able to acknowledge the realities of the new workplace. A deep longing for a return to the past is quite normal. Many people describe their old companies as communities that had values they believed in. This loss of community hurts them so profoundly that they are often unable to plan for the future. Their outrage and confusion have no end (Heckscher, 1995, p. 8).

Although the old order was not ideal, it was seen as fair. Downsizings and reorganizations have destroyed the perception of fairness. For some individuals it has been replaced with intense feelings of imbalance and injustice (O'Reilly, 1994a, pp. 44–45). As their companies have responded to increased competition and to pressures to improve stockholder equity, they feel that their needs have gone by the wayside. A manager in a manufacturing plant explains it this way, "Three to five years ago, I felt pretty close to being comfortable, but now I think I'm part of a big wheel that's just rolling; . . . whatever that wheel wants to do, it's going to do it" (Murray, 1995, p. A1).

These people will never again feel the same loyalty for any job or employer. They are mourning the loss of that sense of belonging, "that feeling of being part of something familiar, special, and unique; of participating in a meaningful, fulfilling, ongoing experience called community" (Zemke, 1996, p. 25). Sue, a programmer at a large financial institution, had to downsize her department and was forced to fire some talented people who were also good friends. She explains that everyone in her organization knows that relationships and the work environment will never be the same again. She thinks that everyone in her company is hurting.

Individuals who lose their jobs are often stunned and shocked. One manager describes it this way: "When my boss told me my job was being eliminated and that I needed to pack my belongings and leave immediately, I felt numb. Although I had been watching my friends leave, I never thought it would happen to me. I put the last sixteen years of my life into boxes. I just walked around in a daze, like I was run over by a steamroller. It took months for the shock to wear off. I think I was better off when I couldn't feel anything. Now I just feel scared and inadequate all the time."

Those who remain in organizations are also in pain. Joseph, a vice president of business development in a biotech company, had to let a third of his department go. Some of his peers also left. He tells us that for weeks people were horrified; they could not believe the magnitude of the changes. The company had lost some very good, versatile people. Most of all, everyone had lost confidence and trust in the management and in the organization. Their reward for staying was more work and longer hours. And they were supposed to be grateful for having a job! Morale was quite low. "I realized that I also was having trouble adjusting to the new rules," Joseph said. "I felt that things were in chaos. I dreaded going to work, whereas before I loved my job. No matter what I did, I just could not feel better. Finally I left."

## Embracing Change

> Free Agents in the marketplace are individuals who are committed to their craft. What is important is the value they bring with them. The Free Agent is a model that is only going to gain momentum as corporations realize how much they need and want these people on their teams.

When the old contract prevailed, people were often expected to give up a great deal of independence in return for security and community. This expectation created corporate environments that were structured and controlling. Many individuals felt stifled by the bureaucracy. The organizations called the shots, and people jumped at the chance for financial and employment security (O'Reilly, 1994a, pp. 44–45).

Some individuals are beginning to see that the "good old days" were not that great and that the world has changed. This insight enables them to move beyond their feelings of outrage, sorrow, and betrayal, and to realize that the death of the old contract can lead to exciting opportunities and a new way to work. They begin to understand why career strategies that were successful in the past are no longer effective. They come to accept responsibility for their own employability and financial security. They gain confidence in themselves and their ability to find satisfying work. Before long, they are Free Agents.

Individuals who become Free Agents represent a rapidly

expanding group of workers who by choice or by chance relate to the marketplace in a new, pragmatic way. Charles Handy, a professor at the London Business School, explains that these individuals "rather than scurrying about looking for a corporate ladder to climb or a professional trajectory to follow, . . . develop a product, skill, or service, assemble a portfolio that illustrates these assets, and then go out and find customers for them" (Handy, 1996, p. 26). They understand that their only security is being able to offer and sell the skills and services the market needs and values.

This knowledge gives them the strength and fortitude to determine their own career paths. They are alert to creating and seizing new opportunities. They feel confident that companies can profit from their skills, their focus on customers' needs, their independent attitude, and their productivity. In return for their best output and their significant contribution to the bottom line, Free Agents expect challenging work, recognition of their accomplishments, and the opportunity to build their resumes and to sell their skills. They are looking for a "fellowship and alignment around a common, worthwhile goal" (Zemke, 1996, p. 26).

Free Agents thrive in the new business environment whether they offer their skills and services internally as full-time employees or externally as consultants, freelancers, or part-timers. Those who provide their skills externally as vendors take a more entrepreneurial route. Others prefer a corporate environment because it offers an array of jobs and learning opportunities in one place. All Free Agents acknowledge that "organizations are never again going to stockpile people. The employee society is on the wane. New models are needed, new role players who will make the new ways less frightening" (Handy, 1996, p. 31).

We were first introduced to the concept of the Free Agent in business in the late 1980's by Paul Hirsch, a professor at the University of Chicago Graduate School of Business. Hirsch questioned what the fallout would be of the many mergers and acquisitions that were beginning to occur with increasing frequency. He predicted that companies would no longer look out for their managers, and as a result "it would be important and necessary to think more like 'free agents.'. . . For better or worse, since the caring corporate employer was becoming an endangered species, managers would have to exercise more independence, consider alternative opportunities on a regular basis, and look out more for themselves" (Hirsch, 1988, p. 18).

Historically there have always been Free Agents. The agrarian economy that existed in the United States prior to the industrial era was dominated by independent workers—Free Agents. In that world, farmers, who were in fact Free Agents, brought their produce and livestock to sell in the marketplace. Their financial health depended on their ability to fulfill customers' needs. They had to be self-reliant, entrepreneurial, and hard-working. Only with the advent of the industrial age did people begin to expect job security and to regard their careers as ever-rising spirals. Like our Free Agent predecessors, today you can expect a career filled with peaks and valleys. Your worth in the marketplace will depend entirely on the perceived value you add at every point in time. Free Agents clearly understand this reality and make sure they are always looking for alternative opportunities to expand their value.

## Free Agent Code

> When I am part of a team, I will do anything for the team and for the project. My commitment to my work has never been stronger. I believe that is what makes me valuable in the marketplace.

For many people the term "Free Agent" has a negative and emotionally charged connotation. When asked to describe Free Agents, they use terms such as greedy, cold, ruthless, self-absorbed, and self-interested. They believe that Free Agents give allegiance to no one, that they are ready to walk out at any moment for more money, with no concern for the group or the project, let alone the company (Heckscher, 1995, pp. 141–142).

Contrary to this negative stereotype, the Free Agents we know are people who are committed to their work and to their colleagues, as exemplified in a common code. Free Agents see themselves as:

- Providing value
- Being adaptable and flexible
- Responding rapidly to market and customer needs
- Taking initiative and risks
- Being self-reliant
- Working collaboratively on a team
- Respecting others
- Building community

In addition, Free Agents develop themselves professionally by:

- Identifying and studying new markets for their skills
- Expanding their skill sets
- Searching for challenging and rewarding work
- Identifying and building networks

By adopting the Free Agent code, you are telling the marketplace, "I'm a business partner with integrity. I have a responsibility for working with the organization and the customer, and for attending to my own personal and professional development" (Hakim, 1994, p. 13). Diane, a compensation specialist, knows that she is as dispensable as anyone else in the organization and is neither bitter nor angry. She takes advantage of every chance to learn and stretch her abilities. She develops relationships throughout the organization so that people will know her work and act as her champions. She is always on the lookout for her next project, even while she is committed to her current projects. As her colleagues begin to understand her code, they turn to her for advice and guidance in many areas, including advice on how to succeed in the new workplace.

Diane and many other professionals like her represent the victors in the new world of work. They are individuals who have been able to discard the ideas of guaranteed lifetime employment and upward mobility. The death of the sacred covenant has given them the opportunity to become Free Agents. They are not immune to the turmoil occurring around them, but they are better prepared and able to deal with the insecurity that is plaguing the corporate world. They are determined to be in control of their own employability. By putting their energy into pursuing opportunities that will make them more valuable now and in the future, they are creating a place for themselves in the new economy.

## Corporate Challenge

Corporations are being affected by rapid changes: increased global competition, new technologies, changing customer demands, and increased shareholder expectations. These pressures demand a formula that guarantees high performance and reduced costs. To remain competitive and profitable, companies are discovering that they need to:

- Quickly acquire people with new or different skills and expertise
- Build short-term commitment to corporate goals
- Motivate people who are capable of working together to quickly beat the competition
- Maintain high performance and still have the flexibility to disband and reconfigure teams, and sometimes entire departments

In spite of constant restructuring, many of today's corporations still do not have workforces that allow them to meet these needs. Instead they have lost a vast body of experience and some of their best people. They are left with a workforce that is struggling to do more with fewer resources. Their employees may not have the right skill sets and may feel insecure and uncertain.

To correct this situation, businesses require individuals who can adapt quickly to the new demands and expectations, people who not only have the necessary skills but can deal with change and uncertainty. They want individuals who are searching for the opportunity to work on challenging projects and obtain new skills, rather than looking for long-term employment and security. They want and need Free Agents. The big question facing most companies is how to successfully compete for these individuals.

Those companies that are most successful understand that Free Agents have new and different expectations for their workplace. In return for hard work, creativity, and flexibility, they want opportunities to:

- Learn new skills and new technologies
- Work on significant projects
- Work autonomously
- Obtain the information necessary to make responsible decisions
- Share decision making
- Interact with other talented individuals
- Align personal and organizational values
- Receive recognition for contributions
- Participate in a meaningful, albeit short-term, community

We found that in organizations that are able to meet Free Agents' needs managers are no longer looking for loyal employees, but for people with the right skill sets who view their commitments as temporary and project-focused. Instead of supplying long-term employment, management assumes the responsibility for providing challenges, coaching, a clear vision, common goals, and an environment where people can perform rewarding work. In these organizations there is a "sense not so much [of] being in this together as of working together toward a common purpose. . . . It is a far more contingent and voluntarist form of community than the old; some might say it is colder and less fair. But it can also be seen as less paternalistic, more capable of responding to and developing individual capacities" (Heckscher, 1995, p. 12).

## The New Ethic

> Some companies seem to be doing rather well without loyalty—not because they have managed to create a successful organization with no community at all, but because they have developed the beginnings of a different ethic [Heckscher, 1995, p. 9].

Many enterprising companies are in the process of defining a "new ethic," which has tremendous potential for both individuals and corporations. They realize that a critical challenge is to transform highly skilled, task-focused, mobile individuals into a caring, productive, high-performing community. To do so, they are committing leaders and resources to building Free Agent communities that are based on reciprocity and an acknowledgment and consideration of both corporate and employee needs.

Because companies can no longer offer security and long-term employment, they must find new ways to build community. To achieve this goal, they are attempting to re-create a "new, more civil code of workplace conduct, a code that accepts the realities of the modern world, but holds that we can both cope with the insecurities and create the openness and closeness with one another that facilitates our work and our humanity" (Zemke, 1996, p. 30) by taking a total approach to building a new order. By treating their employees as valuable assets rather than as commodities, they are creating the foundation for a community of Free Agents who combine their skills and expertise to help a company forge ahead.

This book describes a process for making the changes that can help individuals and organizations define and build new workplace relationships and community. As we have seen, the realities of the new world of work are startlingly lucid. Everyone is touched by the enormous upheaval in the way businesses are organized and work is performed. As one technological advance after another takes hold, skills become obsolete and ways of doing business change. No one, employer or employee, can stand still. Kathryn and Wade point the way to the future: individuals need to take charge of their careers and become Free Agents. Likewise, corporations must determine effective ways to develop environments that appeal to Free Agents. This book provides ideas and strategies for making this transition. The next chapter introduces a process that enables people to heal, move on, regain control, rebuild, and define new relationships and community.

Part One

# *Becoming a Free Agent*

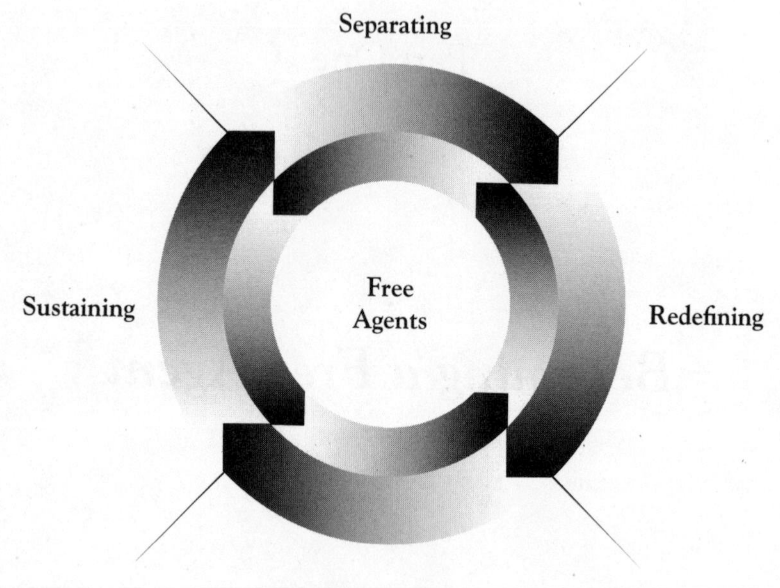
Separating
Free
Agents
Sustaining
Redefining
Positioning

*Chapter Two*

# The Free Agent Process

## Creating a New Future

> At first I didn't realize I was going through a process. All I knew was that I was questioning old assumptions, assessing my strengths and exploring opportunities. It was hard, but it paid off. My best moment was turning down an offer that did not meet my requirements. I knew then that I had become a Free Agent.

Bob was elated when he was named vice president of his company's biggest division. He believed that over the years the organization had given him the freedom to grow. They valued his creativity and leadership. In the fifteen years that he had been there, he had held eight different positions, many of which he had been able to create for himself. He made sure to keep up his contacts with key executives within the company, former colleagues, and his peers in the industry. He aggressively gathered information about new trends both inside and outside the company. If he could continue learning and doing exciting work, Bob planned to stay with the company until he retired. "But if the opportunities to acquire new skills and experiences stop, I'm out of here."

For Jane, a marketing-communications manager, losing a job provided her with the chance to try working for herself. Regaining control of her career had been her long-time dream, but she always gave in to worries about whether she could succeed. Now, she was still concerned but was determined to try. During her corporate career she had specialized in creating marketing-communications materials. She hoped that by going on her own she could do more of what she really enjoyed—coaching executives on their presentation skills. How could she make this dream a reality? She decided to test the market to find out whether the service she wanted to provide was one that potential clients needed. She discovered that it was easier and more lucrative to sell her current expertise. Although she was not able to branch out right away, she realized she could make it as a freelancer. She continues to build and promote her coaching capabilities.

Frank was on the traditional finance career track: graduate school student, accountant, controller, treasurer, and eventually chief financial officer. Along with his financial expertise, he had excellent management and general business skills. But none of that experience mattered when he lost his job during the frantic time of mergers and acquisitions in the late 1980s. The marketplace was glutted with financial managers who had similar resumes, and in interviews he consistently came in second. Frank finally took on some freelance work to support his family while he continued to search for a full-time job. The two years he worked on these projects paid off. He increased his self-confidence, added to his skills, and had current projects and results to sell to prospective employers. When Frank eventually landed a position as chief financial officer in a large organization, he had a much more entrepreneurial and customer-focused perspective. He was more inclined to act as a business partner and try new approaches. Frank is now more valuable than ever; he exemplifies the manager of the future.

While their motivations, situations, and outcomes differ, Bob, Jane, and Frank have all had the experience and benefit of becoming Free Agents. Each of them, with varying degrees of ease, has gone through an accessible process of assuming responsibility for their own careers. From broadening and leveraging their skills to always being alert to new opportunities, they have incorporated the Free Agent process into their work lives. Change is never easy. But Bob, Jane, and Frank agree that the results-oriented Free

Agent process helped them make the transition. The remainder of this chapter introduces and describes this process for individuals. Later in this book we show how the same process serves as a framework for companies to design the foundation for a Free Agent community.

## Becoming a Free Agent

> To prosper in the volatile 1990s, you must be willing to take command of your career. The key is to think of yourself as being self-employed, whether you work inside or outside a company. It's an empowering belief that will help you steer your career and that will influence the quality of your life.

As we help individuals answer the question, "How do I succeed in this new work place?" we tell them that it requires a different approach than in the past. Our experience in helping professionals in a wide range of jobs and functions has led us to identify a fluid and ongoing process that enables people to change. The process has four stages—*Separating*, *Redefining*, *Positioning*, and *Sustaining*—as depicted in the model at the beginning of this chapter.

*Separating.* In this stage you examine your illusions about your relationship to the world of work. You detach yourself from old, ineffective behaviors and beliefs about employment. You begin to make the mental shift from depending on an employer to managing your own career.

*Redefining.* In this stage you identify your past achievements and current desires and goals as a foundation for building your future. You highlight your skills, expertise, preferences, and values. As you examine these, you select and combine the ones that are most important to you to create a Portfolio of Assets—an inventory of what you will be selling in the marketplace.

*Positioning.* In this stage you explore markets for your Portfolio of Assets. You identify current and emerging needs in industries, individual companies, and functions, and match your Portfolio to them. Once you narrow your choices, you begin to sell your skills through networks and alliances that you have been developing.

*Sustaining.* In this stage you commit to remaining a Free Agent for life. You make the decision to continue to do several things: leverage your marketable skills, expand your Portfolio of Assets, identify new and emerging markets and seize opportunities, and maintain and build networks and support systems.

In the following chapters we describe each stage and the means for completing it. We include many examples of how our clients have moved through the Free Agent process. As you will see, although everyone experiences all four stages, there is no clear boundary between one stage and another, and it is common to move backward and forward in the process. Some people go through the process smoothly; others stop along the way to resolve conflicting feelings or to overcome obstacles.

Frank is an example of someone who went back and forth between Separating and Redefining. The first few weeks after he lost his job were more difficult than he could have imagined. He felt demoralized and spent a lot of time alone. It took him a few months before he felt he had conquered his anger about being fired and his apprehension about returning to a cut-throat market. Finally he was ready to do the activities Redefining requires, but every time he felt he was making headway, he fell back into mourning the fact that he had been pushed out the door. Even as he worked on Redefining, he had to continue to detach from the emotions about Separating that were troubling him.

In a static work world, it might have been enough just to become a Free Agent. In a turbulent marketplace, you can never be satisfied with going through the process only once. As a Free Agent you continue to redefine your Portfolio of Assets and position yourself in new markets to be sure that you are always expanding your marketable skills and are poised to spot and seize opportunities. Bob accomplished this goal within his company by seeking eight different positions, each with new skill requirements. Even after Jane had a successful freelance business, she continued to expand her network and seek new alliances, and she was always looking for new applications for her skills.

## Feelings

> It took me a long time at my last job to realize that I needed to leave and that I was hanging on, thinking that I could work things out or that I could be satisfied with less. It wasn't one single incident that caused me to leave. It was more my realizing how little I had going for me there, how little interesting work I had, and how little enjoyment and satisfaction I was getting out of it. It just all came together one day, and at that point I realized I had to get out because there wasn't anything I could do that would sustain me there.

Becoming a Free Agent involves transitions, and transitions are laden with emotion. Even though Jane had wanted to strike out on her own, she went through some rough times. She had a great deal of self-doubt; she worried about her ability to get clients. One day she was elated at the prospect of having her own business; on another, she felt depressed. She was uncertain about what to do next.

The Free Agent process gave Jane direction as well as concrete strategies for learning new behaviors. It highlighted the need to create a financial plan and objectively assess her strengths and prospects. She found the process accessible. It acknowledged the pain she was feeling. She could see that it was a framework for re-creating and persuasively selling herself. It helped her to become a responsible, autonomous agent.

When Andrea came to our practice she was at a low point in her search. She was thinking about getting into a new industry or maybe even a new career. Financially she was still all right, but emotionally she was falling apart. We introduced Andrea to the

Free Agent process, and she was able to reap benefits immediately. Andrea explains:

> The Free Agent process gave me a sense of sequencing. Knowing that there are specific stages and an order for what I need to do is very helpful. It also made me realize that I was not alone— that others are going through the same thing, dealing with the same challenges, and feeling similar ways. The process prepared me in advance for what to expect down the line and enabled me to develop strategies for overcoming potential obstacles. I don't know if it helped me find a job quicker, but it did aid in recovering the sense of worth and value that I had lost.

Regardless of individual circumstances, the process helps people to recognize their emotions. Although some people become Free Agents voluntarily, others are thrown into it totally unexpectedly. Many of our clients tell us that they were shocked when they lost their jobs; they saw none of the signs, and they were unprepared to do anything else. Other people have jobs that they find acceptable but that they know will not meet their needs for the long term. Or they realize that the end of their job is inevitable. They recognize that their opportunities are declining and their options are being cut off. But they worry that they do not have the skills necessary to go elsewhere or that they are too old to make a change. Clients such as these often come to us torn between the intellectual understanding that they must take care of themselves and the emotional desire to be taken care of. They understand intellectually that the workplace has changed, but they find it difficult to change either their skill sets or their approach to work.

These individuals, and even those who eagerly embrace the process for becoming Free Agents, have to deal with intense and often frightening feelings. Free Agents tell us that their biggest fear was not knowing what would come next. Many were leaving behind their jobs after investing years of hard work. Were there any opportunities left? Did they have a future? Jane was lucky; the process helped her realize fairly quickly that her career would continue to grow and develop even though she was giving up job security and a regular salary.

We also see people who fiercely resent having to make a change. As Frank told us, "For twenty years I gave my best, and then I was expected to start all over again. I never thought that at my age I would have to still be proving myself. I mean I did it when I was starting out. But to have to do it now . . ."

Many people find it comforting to know in advance that the Free Agent process is like being on an emotional roller coaster. You can become victimized by your feelings—or energized. You can use them as motivators to help you begin the process, or you can submit to them and use them as an excuse not to change. But you cannot ignore these feelings. In order to become a Free Agent, you need to acknowledge them, experience them, and then move on.

Despite the volatile feelings, the process of becoming a Free Agent can be satisfying. You can enjoy the excitement of trying new projects, choosing what you will do, and being in control of your life. Jane told us that the turning point came for her when she started handing out her brochure and talking to potential clients. Finding that people wanted the skills she had to sell allowed her to leave behind her anxieties and to enjoy the experience of landing her first project.

## Getting Started

> I still had a job—a job I had worked hard to get. And yet I saw what was going on in my industry and in my company. At first I tried to ignore all the warning signs. Soon it was undeniable. I kept trying to get myself started. I thought, if I could just do something to protect myself. But I did not know what to do.

We find that one of the most difficult parts of the process is getting started. One client asked that we "tell people to be quicker to the step than I was. I was too naive, too loyal. I realize now that some situations can't be fixed and have to be scrubbed." From our interviews we compiled some tips to help you begin:

- Acknowledge that you have no choice—that you are going to become a Free Agent.
- Recognize that you may feel anxious and confused. Do not let your emotions stop you from proceeding.
- Use the Free Agent process as your guide.
- Examine your myths about the world of work. Identify and acknowledge those that are no longer effective.
- Find a buddy or ally. A second person can lend much needed objectivity and support.

## Challenges

In the transition to becoming a Free Agent some obstacles have to be overcome. Three of the most difficult challenges are devoting the necessary time, staying focused, and keeping your resolve.

### *Time*

Devoting time to the task of becoming a Free Agent is critical. Bob points out that the process cannot be rushed. For example, you have to scrutinize what you value, what you are good at, and what you enjoy doing. He cautions that you cannot afford to leave any options unexplored or to dismiss any too early. In this process of transformation, he warns, be prepared to move slowly and methodically. This is not the intuitive approach for many people. When in crisis they want to move quickly to a safer place. To get the most from this process you will need to resist flight, slow down, even daydream a little.

Pressure to move more quickly than you should comes unwittingly from friends and family who may ask about progress and results. Explaining the process and sharing small milestones will provide them with the assurance that you are progressing and making good use of your time.

### *Focus*

Keeping your focus on the Free Agent process is important. Find ways to minimize distractions. Many of our clients treat the process as their job and set aside a workplace and regular hours to accomplish it.

Remember that in the Free Agent process the focus is on changing yourself rather than simply looking for another safe haven. Distractions and worries can easily derail you. Anxiety about finances and the emotional upheaval you will be feeling can make you lose focus. In spite of worries and other stresses, it is important to concentrate on the work that needs to be done in each stage.

### *Resolve*

We have found that individuals who become Free Agents resolve that no matter how difficult the process gets they will not slide backward. When Jane first decided to start her own business, she thought that if it did not work out, she could always just get a "job." But then she realized that in order to make her business work she had to be fully committed and intent on never returning to that old relationship. She had to want to be a Free Agent as much as she had ever wanted anything. Eight years later Jane tells us she is glad that she had the tenacity and resolve to continue as a Free Agent.

Frank described how difficult it was to change the way he thought about work. At first, all he wanted was another company to take care of him until he retired. His success in finding freelance work and his realization of how much he enjoyed doing it created Frank's resolve to wait for a position that matched his priorities. He was able to remain faithful to his goal of finding the "right" job because he knew he could do short-term projects for as long as necessary. With this attitude, Frank could be patient and not rush headlong into the wrong slot. He could weigh the pros and cons of the offers he did receive and choose the best one for him.

Sometimes keeping your resolve to continue the process involves celebrating "small wins." In the beginning, activities such as compiling your Portfolio of Assets or researching two new markets will feel like major accomplishments. Later, it is the ability to say no, as Frank did, and wait for the right position.

## Am I There Yet?

When can you be sure you have become a Free Agent? For some, the realization is gradual. For others, the change is quite dramatic. The items in The Free Agent Checklist are a useful benchmark. When you can answer yes to most of the questions, you have made the transition to being a Free Agent.

*The Free Agent Checklist*

_____ I look for opportunities in change.

_____ I accept the insecurity of a job.

_____ I am more vested in challenging work than in job titles.

_____ I see myself as self-employed at all times.

_____ I can clearly describe my strengths and marketable skills.

_____ I am continuously adding to my Portfolio of Assets.

_____ I always look for gaps and needs in the marketplace.

_____ I continuously look for new opportunities to market myself.

_____ I carefully choose new projects.

_____ I am always improving my ability to be a productive team member.

_____ I form networks and alliances to expand my capabilities.

_____ I am committed to remaining a Free Agent for life.

Even when you have become a Free Agent the process will serve as a reminder of what you need to do to remain one. As we have mentioned, this process is ongoing—you cannot afford to stop implementing and refining the strategies that enabled you to set a new course.

## Summing Up

Because it is never easy to change the way we see ourselves and the world around us, becoming a Free Agent is difficult. Some people still do not see the need or are not hurting enough to make the decision to gain control over their careers and their lives. For those who do, the four-step process introduced in this chapter will provide a framework for their transition.

In the subsequent chapters in Part One we explore each of the first three stages in this process—Separating, Redefining, and Positioning. You will hear through the words of our clients what these stages feel like. We will identify the most common pitfalls and obstacles, and provide strategies and activities for moving on.

As with any change, making the decision to do it is the first hurdle. The next chapter, on Separating, will provide some practical ideas for beginning your transition.

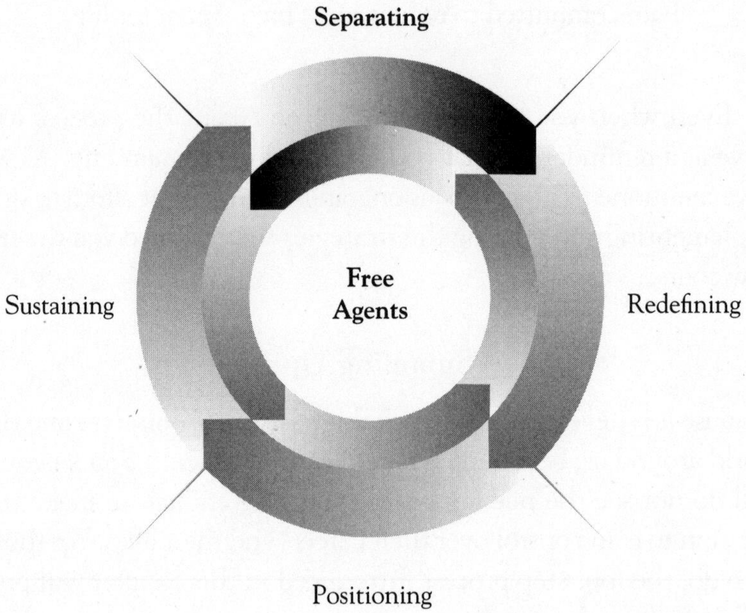

**Separating**

Sustaining

**Free Agents**

Redefining

Positioning

*Chapter Three*

# Separating

## Drawing the Final Curtain

> Every transition begins with an ending. We have to let go of the old things before we can pick up the new—not just outwardly, but inwardly, where we keep our connections to the people and places that act as definitions of who we are.
>
> —*W. Bridges*, Transitions

Roger was doing some serious soul-searching. He was slated to become a partner in a prestigious real estate law firm, but he was finding the system of litigation frustrating and the politics of the firm increasingly difficult to deal with. It was hard for him to admit to himself that he might not want to be a partner. Should he just pull out of a career in which he had invested seven years? Lately he had been thinking that he would rather be in a different environment—maybe a nonprofit organization—applying his law skills in a new way. He would certainly earn less and experience a real upheaval in his life. How could he be sure that would be the right course for him to take? He finally decided that the only way he would ever know for sure was to spend time thinking through his options.

Cynthia heard the words but could not believe them. She had no idea this was coming. But she followed her boss's directions: she spoke with the human resources representative and the outplacement consultant. Then she took her coat and purse and walked out the door as quickly and quietly as possible. She would come back later for her belongings. Although she was in shock, she knew she had to leave with dignity and pride. And she could not cause a scene. She quietly slipped unnoticed out of the building. "Maybe this is just a bad dream," she thought as the door closed behind her.

Although Roger's and Cynthia's situations were quite different, they have joined the ranks of an increasing number of people who are beginning the process of *Separating*, the first step in becoming a Free Agent. Roger, by choice, decided to face up to the fact that his chosen profession might not be the one he wanted forever. He had believed that one chose a profession, attended good schools, secured a position with a reputable firm, became a partner, and enjoyed the rewards forever. For Roger this belief no longer seemed realistic. Cynthia learned that loyal employees have no guarantees. Even though she had worked hard and had been successful, her position was abruptly taken away. Her future will probably not resemble her past.

Roger and Cynthia were not alone in accepting the concept of lifetime employment and the expectation of constant upward mobility. The post–World War II generation did well economically and established a whole new set of expectations. A belief in unlimited opportunity prevailed (Uchitelle, 1994, p. D5). The no-layoff policies of some organizations strengthened these assumptions. Roger, Cynthia, and millions of others, however, are seeing that a new reality has set in:

- The flattening organization does not support constant upward mobility.
- The new skills required for success are different from those required in the past.
- Fewer people are required to perform the same or more work.

Individuals like Roger and Cynthia are profoundly disillusioned. They are realizing that they need to examine their relationship to their work, let go of those beliefs that are no longer valid, and embrace new ones.

Separating is a time of endings and beginnings. It is a time of transitions. Those who are Separating detach themselves from being dependent for their sense of identity on having a specific job in a specific company. They relinquish old mind sets and dated ideas about employment, about how things are supposed to be. They get beyond disillusionment and develop an independence that allows them to take advantage of new experiences and opportunities. As Cynthia describes it, "I am beginning to see myself as a company of one. Finally I know that losing my job was not my fault. It's time for me to adopt a new attitude."

Because Separating is an emotional experience, you cannot simply do it with your head. You need to do it with your heart. Cynthia and Roger experienced the pain and anguish of Separating firsthand. Cynthia was frustrated, angry, and humiliated. She felt that she contributed a great deal over a long time to the organization. She deserved better. She produced good work right up to the minute they told her they no longer needed her services.

Cynthia had to allow herself time to feel angry and hurt. And then she had to make herself move beyond those feelings. She had to realize that her value in the marketplace did not depend on any one company. It was not enough for her to convince herself intellectually. She had to believe it deeply.

Regardless of whether you have been forced out of your job, have left voluntarily, or hold the job of your dreams, you need to begin Separating now. Given the current corporate environment, it is time to change those ingrained beliefs, behaviors, and feelings that turn bright individuals into victims:

- The belief that you will not be affected by current changes in the workplace
- The belief in the idea of lifetime employment and security
- Reliance on your organization to take care of you
- The belief that you will only have to plan your career once

- The fear of not being as successful in the future as you have been in the past
- The fear of being too old to make a change

You can start Separating at any point during your career. Some, especially those for whom the old system worked well, find it more difficult to begin than others. Some realize how the corporate environment is changing and begin the process of Separating immediately. Others grasp the situation intellectually but are unable to act at first. Some wait until an ending is abruptly forced on them. Those for whom Separating is completely elusive give into hurt and bitterness, which paralyze them and prevent them from creating opportunities for themselves.

## Endings

> But all the same, we do find ourselves periodically being disengaged either willingly or unwillingly from the activities, the relationships, the settings, or the roles that have been important to us [Bridges, 1980, p. 93].

As we saw with Roger and Cynthia, Separating involves different kinds of endings. The most obvious ending is the actual physical separation from an existing job. But individuals who remain in their jobs can still experience Separating. In either case, making the psychological shift from being dependent to taking charge of your career and developing options is crucial.

Endings generally fall into two categories, the unexpected and the initiated. This section describes the pain and challenges associated with each of these endings.

### *Unexpected Endings*

You are shocked to discover that you are losing your job. You have seen none of the warning signals and are taken completely by surprise; or perhaps there have not been any signals. You have lost not only your title and position but also your sense of worth and, often, your dignity. Individuals propelled into the stage of Separating by unexpected endings frequently require a long period of grieving before they can make a clean break.

For Cynthia's whole working life she had been making transitions from one position within the company to another. She had made these changes without any difficulty, but losing her job threw her. The loss of security and benefits was difficult. She felt betrayed. She did not know whether she would recover.

### *Initiated Endings*

Reasons for initiating endings vary. You may voluntarily leave your job to take advantage of a new opportunity. Or you may be a manager who needs to change in order to manage other Free Agents. Maybe your work situation has become intolerable, and you are too unhappy to stick it out indefinitely. Or like Roger you may be thinking about making a change and decide to stay where you are only until you sort through your options.

Regardless of the exact situation, you are in the enviable position of starting to Separate while you are still in a job. Because the choice is yours, you will have an easier and quicker separation than those whose ending is unexpected. But you can anticipate going through a period of mourning, pain, and anxiety. After all, you may be leaving behind situations that feel secure and colleagues who are familiar.

## Painful Feelings and Self-Defeating Behavior

All endings by their very nature are painful and disorienting. An ending strips you of everything that is familiar, safe, and comfortable. In addition, when you decide to adopt a new in-charge attitude, you are initiating change, which can be frightening. The known is always more inviting than the unknown.

Each day when she opened her eyes Cynthia felt fine. "And then I'd remember—I lost my job." A sick feeling began in her stomach. She stayed in bed, thinking how hard she had worked for the company, and she became angry and sad. Or she just wandered around, as if she were looking for something she had misplaced. When people asked her how she was, she told them she was in mourning. Feelings like Cynthia's are strongest for those who have lost their jobs. Individuals who are let go usually feel they did not deserve such treatment. They often feel purposeless and rejected or become physically ill and accident-prone. At first Cynthia felt let down and mistreated by her company. She became increasingly bitter and depressed. She began feeling sorry for herself and withdrawing. For weeks she could not even talk to her closest friends and relatives about her fear of not being able to find satisfying work.

Others, like Jane, whom we met in the previous chapter, feel relieved when they lose their jobs. They realize that being let go will end their inertia and force them to begin a process they had been ambivalent about and unable to initiate on their own.

Individuals who are retained during downsizings may feel both guilty about still having their jobs and frightened about the possibility of losing them in the future. After seeing many people let go, one manager realized that the company was getting rid not only of the deadwood but also of some good people. Would he be next? How could he tell? It was all so arbitrary, how could he reassure the people who were left on his team? He also missed the camaraderie he had had with his fellow workers before. His community was broken. It became increasingly difficult for him to deny that he too would have to change.

Often individuals remain in this state of denial as a form of self-preservation. Denial is characterized by refusing to believe that something is actually happening or becoming frustrated when it does not happen fast enough (Jaffe, Scott, and Tobe, 1994, p. 167). Complacency and lack of urgency are common symptoms of denial and frequently sabotage people's efforts to Separate. Although denial may work in the short term, it is not an effective long-term strategy. Change is certain to occur, and it will affect your situation in one way or another. When people give in to denial, they often end up staying too long in unsatisfactory jobs and lose control of their options.

Fear is another powerful reason for not Separating. Many individuals let their need for security and stability guide their decisions and keep them from changing. Their fears allow them to justify staying where they are and prevent them from seeing their options.

For example, Carol had joined a supermarket chain shortly after receiving her M.B.A. After fifteen years of progressing through the management ranks, she began seeing disturbing changes. The organization went through four major structural realignments in four years. After a while the downsizing became too erratic. Carol felt tired all the time and dreaded going to work. She could not resolve the tension between the deteriorating work situation and her need for financial security. She appreciated the perks she received as well as the power and status. Moreover, she enjoyed her work and she was good at it. So she held on. Only when a project that she was seriously invested in was terminated did she finally leave. Looking back from her new position, she knows that she stayed far longer than she should have.

Our clients suggest that asking yourself the following questions can be helpful in determining whether you are denying the need to change:

- Do you usually feel anxious or stressed when you go to work?
- Do you feel discouraged and overburdened?
- Do you feel increasingly unappreciated?
- Do you sense a loss of creative energy?
- Do you feel empty inside?
- Do you feel lethargic and tired all the time?
- Do you find yourself consistently impatient with people?
- Do you feel like staying in bed and not going to work?
- Do you have trouble sleeping or eating?

Some additional questions relate directly to how you perceive your work situation:

- Do you see yourself as being overloaded and ignored?
- Do you find your work less satisfying than it used to be, and do you question its value?
- Do you think your job is a dead end?
- Do you believe that you are unfairly compensated?
- Do you believe that your work is dull and uninspiring?

If you have answered several of these questions in the affirmative, like Carol, you may be struggling with accepting the need to begin Separating. Refusing to recognize the emotions described in these questions often results in carrying excess baggage that prevents you from making progress. Your goal is to move from feeling victimized to gaining a sense of ownership of your new beliefs and behaviors. When you can finally do so, you will be drawing the final curtain.

Roger explained that as he acknowledged his feelings he was able to put himself in the driver's seat and sort through his options. He began to feel much better and more confident, even though he was still uncertain about the outcome and had a lot of anxiety about it.

Regardless of your situation, while you are on the emotional roller coaster of Separating, it is easy to get caught up in some self-defeating behaviors. The following list describes some pitfalls you need to guard against:

- Being immobilized
- Lowering work standards
- Losing commitment to the organization
- Criticizing your colleagues or company (or both)
- Being consumed with anger

- Losing self-confidence and self-esteem
- Tying your identity to your work
- Withdrawing
- Accepting the first offer to join a new team or company

These pitfalls cause problems because they prevent you from continuing on to the next stage of the process. Although our clients tell us that it is easy to fall into these traps, they also agree that recognizing an ineffective behavior is frequently enough to stop it.

If you get stuck, one useful technique is to ask yourself, "How can I use this negative behavior in a constructive way?" For example, rather than criticizing your former colleagues, turn your attention to what you learned from them. If you find yourself questioning your abilities and competencies, think about all you accomplished in your previous position. If you are withdrawing, force yourself to seek out someone to talk to.

Try to turn your anger and self-doubts into motivators for becoming a Free Agent. You can do this by acknowledging your honest feelings, seeking out feedback and support, and separating illusions from truths and facts. Talk to people who know you and look again at past performance reviews. Try to compile an objective picture of your abilities.

Clients tell us that you need to fight against old messages such as "This is the only job I could ever do" and "Why would anyone want to hire someone my age?" You can overcome these messages by acknowledging your limitations and balancing them with your strengths. Another way is to turn the self-doubt around. For example: "I am fifty-eight years old and these are the benefits I bring with me—experience, maturity, and leadership." "They need me because I have twenty years of experience in this industry, I know many of the key players. I have led large teams, and I engender confidence."

Roger had to confront his doubts constantly. Would he be able to give up the partnership for work that paid less? How sure could he be that he would find another application for his skills? Would he be able to find satisfying work? In order not to become his own worst enemy, he had to balance his worries with facts and reality: he was in a position to trade income for personal satisfaction; opportunities for lawyers did exist in many other settings; even though hiring was tight, he was a competitive candidate. When he began to feel unnerved and panicky, reminding himself of these factors helped.

## Skills

Our interviews helped us to identify four skills for letting go of traditional ways of thinking about employment and for successfully integrating new ideas: being open, listening, reframing beliefs, and managing your time. They will also help you free yourself if you fall into any of the traps we just mentioned.

### *Being Open*

Become willing to discuss your concerns and fears about Separating with others. It helps to find people who can listen well and provide an objective view. The individuals you turn to can be those who have made successful endings themselves or people with whom you can share your deepest feelings. If you are generally reluctant to talk about yourself and your emotions with others, you may find being open a challenge.

Roger, a private person, describes the rewards of being able to be open. "I don't usually discuss my feelings. I find it embarrassing to talk about myself in that way. But I could not keep it all inside; there was just too much going on. I went to a good friend and explained my situation. Little by little, his empathy and understanding loosened me up. Talking about what I was going through freed me from the past and let me look toward the future."

### *Listening*

Openness needs to be accompanied by listening. You need to be able to hear and take in suggestions and other important information. Hearing about how others have gotten through this experience and how they were able to change will move you along. It is also important to understand how other people view you. Cynthia explains, "When you are going through a layoff, you tend to think it is your fault, and you put the blame on yourself. You lose your self-esteem and feel unappreciated." When Cynthia began listening to people she respected, she realized that she had many positive attributes. As she began to feel better about herself, she became motivated to start working her way through the process.

### *Reframing Beliefs*

Reframing allows you to look at your situation as an opportunity rather than as a loss. When you reframe old beliefs, you see yourself through a different lens; the focus is on your successes and accomplishments. By reframing, you become your best friend rather than your worst enemy.

The messages we continually give ourselves are called self-talk. Make sure that your self-talk is positive. Constantly remind yourself of past successes. Try not to get the "woulda-coulda-shoulda blues." If your self-talk is all negative, consider it a wake-up call to come to terms with the feelings that are weighing you down. Remember that you owe yourself the chance to find those opportunities that will get you what you want.

Reframing is especially useful for individuals who are currently working. The longer you have been in a position, the more likely it is that your colleagues see you in a specific, fixed way. Over time you tend to see yourself and your options in that same limiting way. A big part of Separating is freeing yourself from these kinds of constraints.

Roger tells us that he needed to start visualizing himself differently. He was stuck because he could only think of himself as a litigator—a person who could get the facts, use them aggressively, and win the cases for his clients. Talking to those he trusted and who knew his work gave him a different picture. He was a strong negotiator, mediator, and project manager. And he was exceptional at planning for unexpected contingencies. As he saw himself in this light, he began to make some progress.

### *Managing Your Time*

Free Agents manage their time well. You need to motivate yourself into action when you are trying to Separate. Allow time every day to think—to confront yourself. Do not allow yourself too much opportunity to wallow in self-pity. Sketch out a schedule to keep yourself moving. If you are working, be realistic about the time you will be able to spend on this project.

## Strategies

> The toughest thing was disengaging from my job and company. I was stunned by how much my self-image and self-esteem were tied to my position. I need to get my sense of self-worth from the work that I do rather than from a title or from being part of an organization. This has been a real struggle for me.

Whether you have a job that is secure or are in danger of losing your job or have recently entered the ranks of the unemployed, now is the time to work through the Separating stage so that you can move on to some challenging beginnings. Separating is difficult. The following strategies enabled our clients to work through this stage quickly rather than wasting time resisting the process.

### *Create a Financial Plan*

It is hard to work through the process when you are worried about finances. Free Agents need to have the financial ability to allow themselves to consider options. They may need time to make the right choice or to find the best project. Free Agents can afford to take risks because they plan their finances for interim and long-term stability.

You can start obtaining control over your finances by detailing your financial needs. Look at your ongoing and fixed expenses, such as housing, child care, and credit-card payments, and determine ways to reduce them. Curb elective expenses, such as entertainment, clothing, and vacations. Many of our clients find it essential to set up a contingency fund to help them through the "drier" times. Every month they put aside a certain amount, even if it is small. This fund increases their financial flexibility.

Cynthia had difficulty dealing with finances. She made the mistake of going through her severance pay and some of her savings before she and her husband scrutinized their finances. They were startled to find that they could cut so many items without feeling deprived. They began their own contingency fund, and they maintain it even though Cynthia has found a new position.

### *Obtain Professional Career Guidance*

Sometimes individuals find it difficult to go through this process on their own. If you find this to be the case, we recommend working with a professional. A career consultant will help you get back on your feet quickly.

Roger at first tried to think through his options on his own, but he found it a struggle. A counselor helped him uncover the deep-seated convictions that were preventing him from Separating and keeping him from moving forward. Being able to talk to a professional confirmed his decision to leave the firm. Ultimately he established a legal consulting firm for nonprofit organizations.

It is also helpful to have someone who can keep you on track. Cynthia's counselor prodded her; he knew when to tell her to stop procrastinating.

### *Find Support*

Regardless of whether you currently have a job, follow Cynthia's example. She found a group of people she trusted who were going through similar experiences. They met regularly to share their feelings. Cynthia was glad to know that she was not alone. Her support group quickly became a replacement for the work group that she had left.

If you decide to become a Free Agent while you are still employed, it is especially important to have people you can talk with openly. You might be able to assemble a group of people who are also going through this process within your organization. Or you may feel more comfortable going outside of your company or even your industry. The important thing is to feel safe and comfortable talking about what you are feeling.

### *Take Care of Yourself*

While you are Separating, you need to give yourself special attention and nurturing. No one can do it for you. Keep yourself in shape mentally and physically. Take advantage of any extra time you have. Exercise. Eat right. Sleep well. Do something daily that you enjoy and that is good for you. Be kind to yourself. Begin the hobby you always wanted to try but never have had the time for. Read those books you have been saving. Part of the Separating process is rediscovering and reclaiming yourself.

### *Develop an Action Plan*

This is a critical time for forging ahead. You have some important decisions to make. Although you may not be in an office every day, you still have work to do. Here are some suggestions for actions you can take.

Whether you are currently employed or not:

- Discuss your current situation with an accountant, financial advisor, attorney, or other professional and develop a financial plan.
- Find a buddy or support group and, if necessary, a career consultant.
- Develop a daily and weekly schedule and action plan to keep yourself on track.
- Keep family members abreast of your activities.
- Exercise and eat a balanced diet.
- Have fun! Reward yourself for your hard work.

If you are not employed:

- Set up a work space for this transition period; obtain equipment and supplies.
- Share the fact that you are no longer employed with your inner circle of friends. Enlist their help and support.
- Get out of the house and meet with people. Make breakfast, lunch, and dinner appointments.
- Treat the Free Agent process as important daily work.

## Moving On

> To leave behind your old expectations—the idea that your employer will take care of you and the notion that a job well done ensures a job forever—is asking a lot, especially when it causes so much dislocation. But the liberation that comes from doing it—that is the light at the end of the tunnel.

Separating is not easy. Individuals persevere and make it through when they realize that responsibility for their career and personal success is theirs alone. Ultimately they are able to disengage from limiting routines and past beliefs. They are able to adapt new, dynamic strategies for success. With a positive, open attitude these individuals find the courage and strength to forge through the Separating stage.

Many of our clients have found the following two exercises helpful as they move through the Separating process.

1. Write down and analyze the following information:
   - The fears that are holding you back
   - Your outdated beliefs and behaviors
   - Your limiting self-talk messages
   - New beliefs and attitudes that you need to adopt in order to move on
2. Develop a contingency fund by
   - Reviewing your existing budget or creating a new one
   - Identifying areas where you can cut expenses such as by renegotiating debts, reducing overhead, cutting back on credit-card usage
   - Revising your budget to include a contingency fund so that it becomes a monthly fixed expense

You can tell that you have progressed through the Separating stage when you can

- Talk to people about your current situation
- Discuss your feelings openly and honestly
- Listen carefully to and act on feedback
- Start believing that you owe yourself the chance to find and pursue new opportunities
- Turn your negative self-talk into positive messages

Many people find it extremely difficult to continue to the next stage, Redefining, until they have successfully adopted new attitudes and behaviors. For others, though, the process of Redefining helps them finally to Separate from old, ineffective beliefs and practices. The next chapter describes how you can Redefine yourself in the marketplace and develop a valuable Portfolio of Assets.

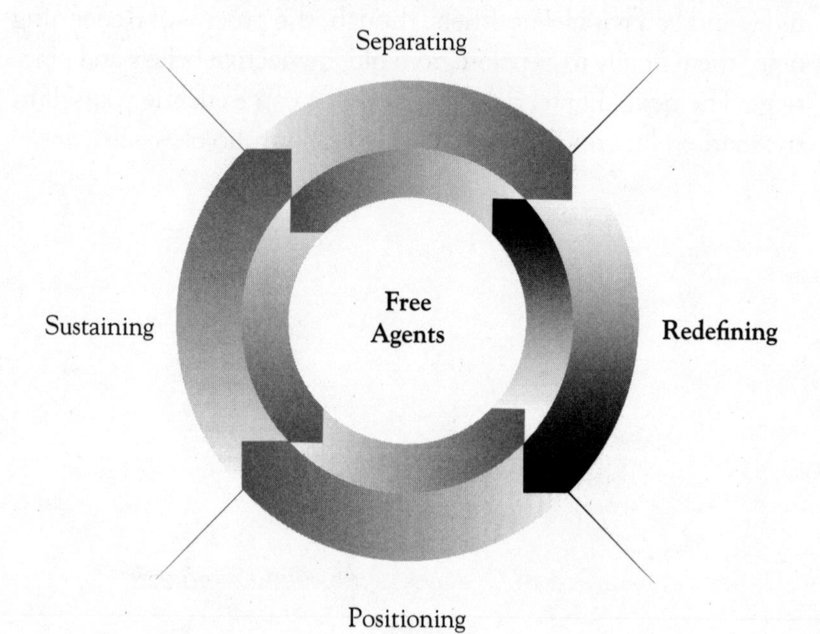
Separating
Free
Agents
Sustaining
Redefining
Positioning

*Chapter Four*

# Redefining

## Moving Beyond Comfort

> Once you make up your mind that it is really over, being able to look forward to the future, rather than looking back, is key to moving on. There was nothing I could do to change what had happened to me, but there was everything I could do to create my future.

Over twenty years ago Dave left graduate school with an advanced engineering degree and joined the management ranks of a farm-machinery manufacturing company. He felt he was on a rocket to the moon until his career was stopped by something he had no control over—corporate politics. When the new CEO brought in his own management team, Dave was passed over for advancement. Although he knew better, he took the whole experience personally. This was an unexpected emotional hit, and it hurt. *Redefining* turned things around for him. As he took a long, hard look at what he did well and what he liked doing most, he was able to get beyond the hurt and come to a surprising realization. Neither money nor security was as important to him as being a major player in the power structure. He had merely been in the wrong place at the wrong time. The skills that had once propelled him in his career were strong and still valuable in the marketplace. He was ready, and it was time to try again.

Redefining makes you look seriously at your accomplishments, your abilities, and your priorities. When you are busy with your job and everything seems to be going well, you probably do not take stock of yourself in this way. And even if you want to, it is hard to know where to start. Redefining requires you to go inside yourself, to determine what you really enjoy doing—not what others want you to do. As a result of Redefining we have seen clients make major moves—from architect to multimedia producer, for example—while others fine-tune their careers. As long as you are honest, you have nothing to lose.

Redefining can feel disruptive at first; the process forces you to be introspective and to be open to new ways of seeing yourself. It pushes you beyond your comfort zone to look at the positive and the negative and to make critical decisions. Basically, Redefining involves using the past to build your future. You redefine, or re-create, yourself by identifying and synthesizing past and current skills, experiences, aptitudes, and interests. You select the ones you want to include in your Portfolio of Assets, which you will be presenting to the marketplace.

Many of us do not look closely at our skills, motivations, and interests in the course of our careers. Successful in a specific position or functional area, we assume we will just ripen with time and maturity. That assumption is no longer valid. Today you need to bring to any position the most up-to-date skills, talents, and specialties. Your security now is in your Portfolio of Assets. When you are clear about your skills and expertise, you can find new and different applications for them.

## Obstacles

> If a man begins with certainties, he shall end in doubts; but if he will be content to begin with doubts, he will end with certainties [Francis Bacon].

Redefining requires a determination to be open to possibilities. There are no simple answers and no overnight successes. People who have always had all the answers find it difficult to go back and start with the questions that need to be answered in the Redefining stage.

Before Redefining, Gloria, a senior marketing manager for a large consumer-product company, was feeling dissatisfied with her current position. She had tired of working for a large organization and wanted to acquire some skills and experience that broadened her sales and marketing expertise. But where and how? Should she move to another company with a different product line? Would it be better to get some operations experience? She felt scared and uncertain. As she began Redefining, she realized that she had neglected to ask herself the most important questions of all: What did she want to do next? What were her goals? She needed answers to these questions before she could plan her next steps.

Redefining is hard work, and many people will lose the path at this point. As at any other stage in becoming a Free Agent, it is easy to get stuck. Some of the most common obstacles are continuing to see yourself as others do, carrying forward bitterness and anger, and becoming impatient and discouraged with the process. These obstacles can thwart your efforts and prevent you from getting the information you need to be able to make vital decisions.

Everyone would have been amazed had Jesse not followed his father and grandfather in becoming a physician. After five years in a multispecialty group practice, he became disenchanted. Although he assumed much of the administrative and management responsibility for running the group, he still was not satisfied. In spite of his natural proclivity for administration, his internal messages kept him from making a move. Through talking with mentors and getting in touch with his desires and preferences, he was able to put the old "oughts and shoulds" to rest. He gave himself permission to resign from the practice and enroll in a full-time master's degree program in health care administration.

As you go through this stage, you may find that you are still feeling angry and bitter—emotions that can be either motivating or debilitating. Once again, the sooner you get in touch with your feelings, the greater chance you have of gaining control.

You may get discouraged and want to stop. Here, your perseverance will be tested. Dave admits that he got impatient with Redefining. He needed a lot of encouragement from his family and friends. In the end, he realized how important it was that he had answered all the questions in this stage in order to be able to figure out what he wanted to do next. He would not have reached this point if he had not taken the process seriously or had quit halfway through.

Redefining does take faith. The first rule is to trust your instincts so that you can be sure you are not merely satisfying others' expectations. The second rule is to trust this part of the process. The process works; we have watched our clients go through it successfully over the last decade. Gloria recalls, "It was difficult to work through Redefining, but it forced me to look at what I really wanted and to listen to my responses. At first it was quite frightening; it had been a long time since I was so in touch with myself." When you decide to take this leap, you will be surprised and pleased to find where you end up.

## Strategies

Re-creating yourself requires organized introspection. As you build your Portfolio of Assets, be prepared to investigate new and different paths. Perhaps you will have the same experience as Jesse and find something waiting for you that you do not anticipate. The following strategies are concrete ideas for helping you through this stage.

### *Do Not Look for Shortcuts*

You cannot cut corners in Redefining. It takes time and effort to develop your Portfolio of Assets and shape your future career. There are no quick and facile answers to questions such as: What have I always wanted to do? Am I doing what I want to do? What do other people do that sounds interesting? What have I accomplished? What do I want to do for the next five years?

### *Work with a Coach*

We are often our worst critics but rarely our best judges. If you need help in this area, choose a coach to help you through the process. Your coach can be a professional career consultant or someone else with whom you feel comfortable sharing your past as well as your future aspirations. A coach can also provide help in selecting the components of your Portfolio of Assets. It is easy to edit yourself as you go through this process and omit some important skills. Choose someone who is open-minded and objective and who can provide guidance and understanding.

Dave's story underscores the value of working with a coach. He was confused and unfocused when he was working alone. He thought more about his past experiences than about what he was going to do next. He found it difficult to look at his skills in a positive way. Every time he thought about work he might enjoy, he also thought of all the reasons why he could not do it. His career consultant provided him with the structure, support, and objectivity he needed to move ahead.

### *Seek Out Mentors*

As you go through Redefining, we urge you to talk to people you know and respect who have had an interest in your career. Mentors are familiar with your capabilities and accomplishments; they have seen you in action. They can relate their own experiences in ways that stimulate your thinking. These individuals know you well enough so that they can remind you of successes and skills you might downplay or overlook. And often they know the environments, companies, or industries that might be a good fit for you. Use them as sounding boards for setting priorities and goals for yourself.

### *Trust Your Instincts*

Answers to the questions you will be considering in this stage are not always obvious or in the forefront of your mind. Sometimes you need to go way inside yourself and do some dreaming to find them. Dave finds his instincts to be invaluable allies because they generally give him the right message. He trusts his instincts because he feels that they reveal the collective wisdom of his experience and maturity. Be sure to listen to what people say, but then do what you know is right for you. At this time you are vulnerable, and other people can easily influence your decisions. Guard against being pressured into outcomes that run counter to what you want.

### *Structure Your Time*

Be realistic about the time you have available, and set aside a regular block of time for thinking through the components of your Portfolio of Assets. If you are working, you may not be able to schedule time every day, but be sure you do so on a weekly basis. Set up appointments to meet mentors or to work with your coach. Keeping to a schedule will help you maintain your momentum and expedite results.

## Assembling Your Portfolio of Assets

> Redefining enables you to get yourself market-ready and hone your skills so that they continue to have value in the market. It also enables you to gain control of your life.

Redefining involves assessing your values, skills, special knowledge and expertise, personal characteristics, desires, professional goals, preferred environment, and need for further professional development. In this section we suggest how you can evaluate each of these factors and build your personal Portfolio of Assets.

### *Values*

Because Redefining involves determining what is important to you, the work must begin with identifying your basic values. A value is any quality desirable as a means or end in itself. You can determine your priorities by rank ordering the values in this list:

_____ Creativity and challenge: Taking the initiative to develop innovative solutions and to produce new and original works.

_____ Expertise: Possessing great skill or technique and becoming an authority in a specific area.

_____ Family: Placing family needs above professional needs.

_____ Health: Enjoying and promoting one's physical well-being.

_____ Independence: Having freedom of thought and action.

_____ Leadership: Inspiring others to achieve community or organizational goals.

_____ Leisure: Having enough time to enjoy recreation and nonwork interests.

_____ Recognition: Receiving special public or private notice or attention from superiors and peers.

_____ Relationships: Developing close, trusting work relationships.

_____ Service: Contributing to the community.

_____ Variety: Having the opportunity to work on different activities at the same time and over time.

_____ Wealth: Earning a great deal of money.

Given your priorities, describe how these values affect what you want in your next job. For example, if wealth is most important to you, you need the opportunity for high compensation or an equity position. As you begin to position yourself in the marketplace, you want to be sure that the choices you make are consistent with the values that have your highest ranking.

Identifying their values enables Free Agents to redefine their concept of success. Jane used to think success meant making a lot of money. But in the course of Redefining she realized that she is most happy when she has extra leisure time. "Of course I'd like to make more money—who wouldn't? But that would mean I would have to give up time with my dog, my friends, my sports. Coming to grips with what is really important to me has made it easier to make choices."

### *Skills*

Most of us tend to define ourselves by our job titles and responsibilities rather than by the skills we possess, but employers today are interested in the abilities and expertise candidates will bring to a position or project. Redefining provides the structure and framework for developing this information about yourself and for identifying those skills that are your strongest and that you enjoy the most.

Begin by making a list of at least five major personal and work-related accomplishments—things you did that you are proud of. Describe each item in terms of the problem—what you were trying to do; action—what you did; and outcomes—what happened because of your action.

Note the skills that enabled you to be successful. For example, if in an increasingly competitive marketplace you grew market share by 30 percent over two years, you might have been successful because of your leadership, decision-making, problem-solving, and negotiation skills. Or if within one year of a merger, you built a cohesive work unit with high morale and no turnover, you might have achieved this feat through your communication, coaching, and motivating skills.

Finally, make a list of those skills that you consistently demonstrate and enjoy. These are the skills that you will include in your Portfolio of Assets.

### *Special Knowledge and Expertise*

Everyone has special knowledge and expertise that they acquire from work, community service, and hobbies. Although they may be obvious to others, frequently such knowledge and expertise are difficult for you to identify, and they are glossed over or forgotten. To be sure that you capture significant knowledge and expertise, begin by thinking of everything you enjoy doing or do well. These activities may have been a small part of a past position, or you may have performed them as part of a community-service project or in your leisure time. Next ask your family, friends, and mentors to help you complete your list. Finally, study the list and highlight the areas that you want to include in your Portfolio of Assets.

As many individuals go through Redefining, they reactivate skills they enjoyed earlier in their careers and in their leisure activities. For example, when Theresa thought seriously about what she had done throughout her life, she realized that she had abilities that she had not put on her resume. She spoke two languages fluently; and she was good at synthesizing complicated technical material and presenting it in an easy-to-understand manner. She increased the value of her Portfolio of Assets by adding these abilities to it. She is now a documentation specialist on a software team that is developing a new foreign-language program.

### *Personal Characteristics*

Free Agents have a good sense of the personal attributes that make them effective. Personal strengths are those "soft" skills that you exhibit to a noticeable degree. What are the words that you or others use to describe the "unique" you at work? Our clients have identified such characteristics as inspiring confidence and being enthusiastic, patient, collaborative, fair, intuitive. Evaluate your personal characteristics, identify those that are most descriptive of you, and consider which of them add to your market potential.

### *Desires*

In Redefining, it is important to ask yourself what you want. Often, deep inside ourselves we know what we want, but we have trouble answering the question. Someone may have taught us to ignore our desires, and over time we begin to think of them as fantasies that have no root in reality (Bridges, 1994, pp. 77–78).

Desires are great sources of motivation; they can spur individuals to unbelievable accomplishments. Think about what you will do when you really want something to happen. As W. Bridges reminds us, "People who desire something work long hours; they make sacrifices, they swallow their pride and forget how others might perceive them; they discover talents they never knew they had; they argue their case so persuasively . . . that they gain allies; and they solve problems that in any other setting they would have considered insoluble" (1994, p. 79).

Our clients dig deep within themselves to discover what they truly enjoy doing. They tell us how important it is to find out what makes them passionate about their work.

### *Professional Goals*

Planning for the future involves defining goals by considering your values, expertise, and skills. Use the information you have obtained so far to help you formulate a short list of professional goals you would like to achieve over the next three to five years. Pick the one or two you can realistically achieve. Look carefully for conflicts that may exist between the goals you formulate and the values you think are important. If you identify potential conflicts, develop strategies for overcoming them such as ranking your goals and executing them sequentially, postponing goals that are in conflict with short-term values, or combining two conflicting goals into one that is workable.

Gregg wanted to become expert in the distribution of gourmet food products in Asian markets. He had been offered a position in his company that would enable him to meet this goal; it would require spending at least 60 percent of his time in Asia. His highest value, however, was being with his young children. Obviously, he had a conflict to resolve. He realized that to meet his goal he could either seek out a position based in Asia and take his family with him or he could postpone his professional plans for several years. Being aware of this conflict ahead of time actually enabled Gregg to identify additional options and avoid feeling trapped.

### *Preferred Working Environment and Conditions*

We are often surprised by how little consideration our clients initially give to understanding the conditions that enable them to work best. Most individuals are influenced by their work environment, which includes geographic location, length of commute, amount of travel, physical surroundings, scheduling flexibility, length of workday and workweek, company culture, corporate values, management style, and professional-development opportunities.

Dave almost accepted an offer that he never should have considered seriously. He was taken in by a company culture that appeared to promote trusting and caring relationships. He thought he would be part of an ideal team. He had overlooked the lack of structure and had ignored a leadership vacuum; it was a company in which decisions never got made.

Free Agents are clear about, and look for, those environmental factors they need to be able to perform at their highest levels. Consider your needs and list those that are most important to you. Use them as a checklist when evaluating companies you want to work for or with.

### *Need for Further Professional Development*

In the self-reliant Free Agent world continuous learning and personal development are vital. Free Agents understand the importance of systematically updating their skills to keep ahead of the needs of the marketplace and the demands of new and emerging technologies. At the least, you need to know the latest software applications in your specialty. If you do not keep your skills current, you are sure to be left behind. The deeper and wider your skills are, the more valuable you will be. Even at an early stage, you should be thinking about new skills you may want to acquire. At times it may be advantageous to add skills that will raise your worth to a particular employer. At other times, however, you should focus solely on gaining skills that are more generally transferable. Your decision about which skills to develop should be based on an analysis of the strengths you want to enhance or the weaknesses that limit your opportunities. Make a list and look for ways to develop additional skills even as you work your way through the Free Agent process.

## Final Synthesis

The final task is combining these components into your Portfolio of Assets. In *The Age of Unreason*, Charles Handy describes a portfolio as a collection of items that have a theme; each portfolio is composed of many parts that become a whole. He cautions that careful choice, not chance, should determine the items that you select to tell potential employers about yourself (1989, pp. 183, 191). If you use as criteria both proficiency (what you do well) and pleasure (what you enjoy doing), you will likely make the best choices for your Portfolio.

It helps to synthesize information by having it all in one place. The following exercise gives a comprehensive picture of the components you have been assessing so that you can see patterns and any conflicts that you still need to resolve.

1. Answer the following five questions:

   - What values are most important to me?
   - What skills am I selling?
   - What special knowledge do I have?
   - What are my preferences for my workplace?
   - What are my goals?

2. Write down your highest ranked items in each category.
3. Study the sheet and decide which items to leave in or omit and which lower-ranked items, if any, to add.
4. Rethink the items until you have an integrated Portfolio to test in the marketplace.
5. Use your worksheet to develop a short sound bite that answers the question "Tell me about yourself."
6. Practice your story out loud before relatives and friends.

Redefining yourself and revising your Portfolio of Assets on a regular basis are necessities in today's world. In a skill-driven market, you need to be able to present yourself clearly and articulately. Once you have your Portfolio of Assets, you are ready to look for opportunities to position yourself in the marketplace. In the next chapter, on Positioning, we look at how to identify those markets that are congruent with your values, skills, and goals.

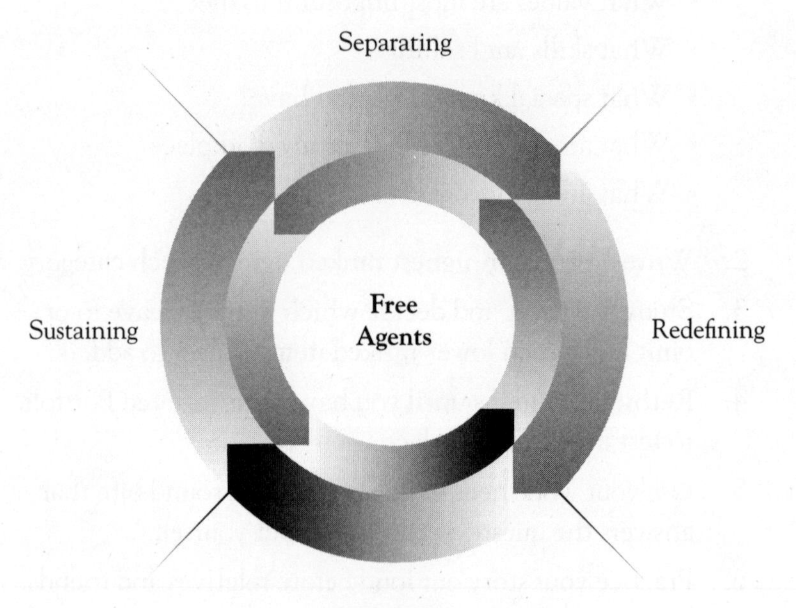
Separating
Redefining
Positioning
Sustaining
Free Agents

*Chapter Five*

# Positioning

## Staking Your Claim

> Essentially what we are doing in this stage is selling ourselves. Intellectually I think I understood that, but emotionally I didn't until I experienced the pain of constantly putting myself on the line and facing rejection. Intuitively it makes sense to look at yourself as a work in process and to identify your core assets and then sell them in the marketplace. The question ultimately is, "Are you willing to do what it takes to get the opportunity you want?"

Jay was restless. He had been in the commercial real estate business over fifteen years, ever since earning an engineering degree and an MBA. His specialties were construction management and site acquisition. For many years he found the work exciting and full of variety. But as the industry declined, his opportunities for a good income and complex deals evaporated. His only choice was to try to leverage his skills in another industry. Two growth industries that interested him were managed health care and telecommunications. He chose to focus on managed health care because he knew people in that industry. After six months of research he realized that the field did not build on his strengths. It would be too big a leap for him.

Jay decided to go on to Plan B—telecommunications. Returning to the library and doing all the necessary new research was tedious. Fortunately, it turned out to be the right market for his skills and personality. He was surprised at how relatively easy it was going to be to transfer and leverage his skills. Within three months, Jay was offered a management position at a telecommunications company.

Ann's story is somewhat different. The idea of selling herself was completely foreign to her. Merit had been her byword. She believed that if you did a good job, recognition and promotions would follow. When the promotions did not come, she was forced to change her thinking. Ann made a 180-degree turn. She identified her assets and developed a strategy for selling herself. She targeted six managers in her own company and an equal number in other companies in the industry for informational meetings. She also volunteered to take on a special project and participated actively in team meetings so that she could get more visibility.

When she focused on potential markets for her skills, she realized that she did not even have to leave her company. During her fifth meeting, she was offered a project-leader position in another unit in the company. Although it was not a promotion, it offered her other benefits: continuing visibility and opportunities to manage people. She is not sure what she will do when this project is over, but she is not as concerned as she would have been earlier because of her new understanding of how to sell herself.

Both Jay and Ann were in the *Positioning* stage of the Free Agent process. In this stage you explore markets for your Portfolio of Assets. You research and identify current and emerging market needs, and match your skills and competencies to them. You examine new industries, businesses, and job functions, or you become more familiar with your industry. Simultaneously you develop networks, alliances, and distribution channels for your Portfolio of Assets. Finally, you narrow your choices and begin to sell your skills. As a Free Agent you can expect to repeat Positioning continuously.

You may be thinking that this sounds like the same old process for "looking for a job." But if you take a closer look, you will see the difference. We are suggesting that you forget about looking for a job. We are recommending that instead you look for a market that will let you apply your skills in a way that creates value for you and for your customer, the organization or the client you want to hire you. In this process you convert yourself into a business, and you find the customers for your Portfolio of Assets (Filipczak, 1995, p. 32). Looking for markets, rather than jobs, is less constricting and frees you to consider a broader range of possibilities.

In the Separating stage, you adopted a Free Agent state of mind. In the Redefining stage, you assessed your skills, interests, and goals. You determined which skills you want to showcase to employers and made some initial choices about which skills to expand and which new ones to learn. In this stage you will be concentrating on finding markets and learning about the opportunities available to you both inside and outside your company.

## Markets

> Looking for a market is a learning process. You need to stop thinking in terms of a job and start searching for applications for your skills. This requires you to understand your core capabilities and how they operate in the marketplace.

In traditional job seeking, as soon as you were handed a pink slip or whenever you wanted to make a change, you made a few phone calls to find out what similar jobs were available or you pounded the pavement offering yourself over and over again. Sooner or later you landed a job. The changes that are occurring in the workplace make this product-driven approach obsolete. Today you need to search for a market where your Portfolio will be valued, and you need to sell those skills to the customer who offers you challenging and rewarding work, the opportunity to contribute, and the chance to learn new skills in exchange for your expertise.

Tony, who was traumatized when he was let go, explained that at first he was feeling desperate, so he networked furiously. He made lots of phone calls, sent out resumes, and made appointments. However, this strategy did not work. It became obvious that he was focused on the wrong thing—just getting the same job in another company. He was stuck looking for titles rather than multiple markets for his skill sets. He had to accept the fact he had to know more about the needs of the marketplace and be more articulate about how his skills could meet those needs.

Tony and many other clients tell us that Positioning alters their perspective. They now look beyond their jobs to the marketplace. They stay on top of their businesses, their industries; they look for new trends, emerging markets for their skills, and industry needs. They are always ready for a move within their company or outside. Ann tells us that because she knows in the back of her mind that she may get a pink slip at any time, she is always looking for new markets for her skills. This new perspective gives her a decided edge in her own company because more than others she studies and gains insight into the competition, new trends, and customer needs and expectations.

In *JobShift*, Bridges devotes an entire chapter to the significance of looking beyond the confines of a job. He discusses the power of viewing the entire work marketplace. This is where Free Agents operate. They are market-driven and understand that constantly assessing the marketplace is critical, that the products and services provided by businesses are changing rapidly, and that these changes create new needs that represent opportunities for them (1994, pp. 61–75).

In the marketplace of work Free Agents are the suppliers or sellers, and they are seeking buyers or customers. The goods and services they are exchanging are their skills, experience, and competencies—their Portfolio of Assets. Free Agents understand that in a marketplace there is an exchange of goods of equal value and that value is determined by what sellers think their goods are worth and by what customers are willing to pay. Free Agents study this arena to understand the supply and demand situation, which determines their value. Because they know they need to create interest, value, and demand, they understand the importance of differentiating their product, staying on the cutting edge by anticipating change, recognizing trends, and being ready to meet new business needs.

At the same time, businesses and industries are changing to meet competition by offering new goods and services. These changes create new needs and thus new opportunities. Free Agents learn to look for these opportunities and to capitalize on them. They define niches and turn unmet needs—or gaps—into opportunities (Bridges, 1994, pp. 67–69).

Free Agents within companies describe how they routinely spot gaps and make the case for their ability to meet them. Many of our clients have created entirely new slots for themselves or added an unexpected and challenging function to their job description. They aggressively identify emerging applications for their skills and competencies.

Lourdes, a manager, said that when she returned from maternity leave, the company offered her a position that she did not want. After some investigation, Lourdes discovered that the company wanted her in that position for her coaching and motivating skills. She immediately wrote a proposal showing how those skills could be more useful to the company in their new telesales department. She could effect results by coaching front-line telesales representatives in consultative sales skills, and she could work in a department that she believed was important to the company's future. Management was impressed with her research, knowledge of the business, and tenacity. They approved her proposal and created the position for her.

## Stresses and Strains

> You start to think, "Where is this going to end? Will I ever find work as interesting and satisfying as what I have been doing?" And you can't imagine what it would be, no matter how hard you try. What I've learned from this experience is that you can't be impatient; new opportunities will come along. It's just amazing that I've ended up here. But I would never, never have expected it.

Positioning is a period of great energy output and activity characterized by both uncertainty and creativity. Many people become intoxicated with possibilities and opportunities. Others become overwhelmed. Your brain will constantly be on fast forward. You may feel elated and invigorated as well as frustrated and depleted.

As you work your way through Positioning, it helps to remind yourself that this stage, like the others you have been through, is not linear. There will be detours and reversals along the way. Many people use it as a time to integrate their lives. Ann saw it as a critical developmental stage. She was aware that her six-year-old was going through predictable developmental phases, but she was surprised that she was. Being unable to anticipate what she was going to be doing next was unsettling. Until she found a new market for her skills, she felt out of control. Watching some of her friends and peers work through the same process was comforting because it made her realize that opportunities present themselves unexpectedly.

Anxieties abound. How long will my money last? Is this opportunity really good for me? When will my life be back together again? Will they hire someone my age? But if you become overwhelmed with anxieties, both financial and personal, you may become paralyzed. Or you may accept an offer too soon or take too narrow a view and not see all the possibilities. You need to protect yourself against caving in to your fears and worries.

Rosemary, who had been let go with three months' severance pay after spending her career in medical-equipment sales, was making great progress in becoming a Free Agent. She was eager to work on her Portfolio of Assets and research new areas for her skills. Her goals were to remain in sales with a company that was the market leader in the industry. She wanted an environment that would support her consultative sales approach. She spent her days making new connections, talking to people, and identifying potential companies and products. Some leads led nowhere, while others were fruitful. Finally her efforts led her to a company that sounded like a good match. After spending many hours meeting with people in the organization and satisfying their candidate profile, she was offered the position of strategic account manager.

It was an appropriate and timely offer that could help Rosemary make the transition into a new product area. Her severance period was nearly over, she was increasingly anxious about her finances, and this was her only offer. But something bothered her. She reviewed her notes and weighed the pros and cons of this position. Finally she decided that she had to follow her instincts. Even though she was scared about her future and especially her finances, she knew in her heart that this was not the right place for her. The issues that concerned her were not negotiable and went to the core of the company. When she was honest with herself, she admitted that other companies had better products and that this company was not committed to providing the necessary technical support.

After refusing the offer, she fought feeling let down and continued to follow up on her referrals. Within a month she was offered, and accepted, another position that was much better aligned with her goals. As she explains, "If I had not waited and had given into my anxieties, I would have missed a wonderful opportunity. It was terribly difficult, but I learned to focus on what is important to me. I feel a lot stronger as a result of my ability to conquer my fears."

Getting bogged down in this part of the journey is another danger. Some people have difficulty eliminating options and making decisions, while others become immobilized with too much information. For those individuals the end point becomes collecting information rather than finding a market. If you do get stuck, it helps to remind yourself that there is a beginning, a middle, and an end to this stage and there are some specific skills that can help you along the way.

## Skills

Free Agents find that sharpening some skills makes working their way through Positioning easier; these skills are doing thorough research, being able to listen well, and staying focused.

### *Doing Research*

Research involves gathering as much information about markets as you can. It includes talking with people, reading print materials, using the Internet, and investigating other sources of pertinent information. You are looking for several different kinds of information about an industry, company, or market: history, key players, key technologies, general health, trends and future directions, unmet needs, barriers to entry and competition, income opportunities, and skills required. Be sure you collect the same type of data on each market you research.

Here are some specific questions you want to ask:

- What are the long-term trends and needs in the industry?
- What are the areas of growth and decline within the industry?
- What new technologies are playing a role in shaping the industry?
- What will future job opportunities look like?
- How could my skills add value now and in the future?
- What are the opportunities for leveraging my current skills?
- What is the earning potential for someone with my skills?
- In what areas do I need further professional development?
- How can I establish credibility in a new industry or job?
- What skills or value does my competition offer?
- How do I develop expertise quickly?

Concentrating on finding answers to these key questions allows you to accumulate a lot of data quickly by streamlining the information-gathering process.

### *Listening*

In Positioning, as in Separating, listening is an indispensable skill. Probably all of us can improve in this area. When you are interviewing people to obtain information about markets, pay careful attention to both what is and what is not being said. Listening to the answers is as critical as asking the right questions. Tune in to the subtle, nonverbal messages you receive. Preparing your questions ahead of time will help you pay attention, listen, and observe carefully. After interviews, ask yourself these questions:

- What did their body language tell me?
- What did their words tell me?
- How receptive were they to my Portfolio?
- What concerns did they express?
- What advice did they offer?
- How should what I heard and observed influence my decision?

Larry had been a branch manager for a large bank for many years. He saw branches being eliminated, knew his could be next, and thought he could become the manager of any small retail business. He spoke to many people, but he blocked out what they were saying. Had he listened, he would have realized that he was being told that his skills were not readily transferable to just any business. Instead, he subjected himself to constant rejection. He stayed in this painful place until he was able to take in the feedback he was getting. He eventually heard the message and successfully made the lateral switch to manager of a small niche bank.

### *Staying Focused*

You can easily become swamped with the vast amount of information that is currently available. But you must keep your focus. You are on a mission to discover as much as you can about present and future changes and needs in specific industries and companies. Do not lose sight of what you are looking for. Weeding out extraneous and irrelevant information makes it easier to analyze and synthesize your data.

Jeanie, an industrial designer, wanted to start her own business. While still employed, she went through several months of intensive market research hoping to spot the next "waves"— niches that would be "hot" in the future. She studied all the information she could find about demographic shifts and the needs such shifts would create. Keeping herself focused, she was able to come up with an array of new-product ideas, which she narrowed to a product line for aging baby boomers.

## Strategies

> In the end I found that my "homework" not only led me to the right customers but also sent the message that I was motivated. In every interview people picked up on the fact that I had taken the time to research the industry and to match my skills to their needs. I was the winner!

Doing your homework will let you know exactly who the customers for your Portfolio of Assets are, what these customers want, and how you can give it to them (Filipczak, 1995, pp. 31–32). We recommend the following strategies to help you identify your markets and your customers.

### *Be Methodical*

It is critical to think about systems for organizing the data you will be gathering and to decide ahead of time which system will work best for you. It is self-defeating to have no way of managing or retrieving the data you have collected. The goal is to obtain information that you can easily find and use. Some people use index cards or loose-leaf notebooks; others enter the data on a computer. Whatever system you choose, you must have the ability to sort across various categories, such as industries, companies, individuals, job functions, geography, and technologies. As you read and talk with people, you need to collect parallel data. Ask everyone the same basic questions. Then when you analyze the data, you will be comparing apples with apples.

Jay's approach was to rely heavily on computerized data and informational interviews. He thought he was being systematic about his research. About midway through he tried to compare the sales figures for two different segments of the market and found that he did not have the data he needed. He looked at the notes from his meeting with the sales manager of Company B and was chagrined to discover that he had asked a completely different set of questions than he had at Company A. It was a sobering lesson.

### *Build and Maintain Networks*

When you are searching for markets, you can never talk with too many people. Your business and personal acquaintances can provide you with important information and open doors for you. Talk with others who are successful in their work and who have a broad view of their company or industry. Try to leave the door open to return for more information, referrals, or suggestions.

A network has many components: friends, college classmates, members of social and professional organizations, past employers, suppliers, vendors, colleagues, and mentors. It even includes people you may not know who share common affiliations such as sororities and fraternities, undergraduate and graduate schools, social clubs, and religious organizations. Expanding a network can be done in numerous ways—for example, targeting and seeking out people in other divisions of your company or industry, serving on company committees and working on company service projects, serving on professional and nonprofit committees and boards, volunteering in your community.

The more people you talk with and the more times you describe your skills and what you would like to do, the greater is the likelihood that you will hear about opportunities or get referrals to people who can be helpful. Our clients have found that their inner circle is the most eager to help, but their outer circle, those whom they do not know, are most likely to connect them with opportunities. If you visualize this process as one of moving further and further out on the limbs of a tree, it is those people farthest out who may be the most helpful. Your job is to make enough connections so that you reach that outer group. Many clients are surprised at the large number of strangers they talk to during this stage. But they assure us that during this stage they feel the most energized and engaged. They often meet people with whom they build personal relationships and continue to network and brainstorm.

As you talk with people you will want to develop a system for tracking your conversations. In addition to mentioning to our clients the many good software packages that are now available, we share with our clients the sample worksheet presented in Exhibit 5.1.

You will find that some people are willing to talk and others are not. The best salespeople know that if you are never rebuffed, you are not asking enough people. Building these connections is probably the most important strategy in the Positioning stage. Free Agents realize that they have to expand their networks and talk with people all the time.

Jay was intrigued with networking. He found it amazing that people would make themselves available for informational interviews, particularly in December. It turned out that December was a good month to meet with people because they tended not to travel as much and many offices were more relaxed during December than at busier times of the year. Jay found that people were willing to take time for him and he usually had two additional referrals each time he finished an interview. If he had been trying to get a "hard" interview and an offer, however, December might have been a difficult time.

### *Check Out Hypotheses*

As you do your interviewing, check out your developing hypotheses and ideas about how you would fit into an industry or company.

**Exhibit 5.1. Conversation-Tracking Worksheet.**

Name:

Company/Title:

Address:

Phone/Fax/e-mail:

| Actions | Date | Notes | Follow-Up Steps |
|---|---|---|---|
| Called/left message | 5/2 | Out of town until next week. | Call back 5/11. |
| Talked on the phone | 5/11 | Finally, we connected. Will have breakfast meeting on 5/14. | |
| Met for breakfast | 5/14 | Had some interesting information and ideas. Gave me some referrals. Impressed with Portfolio. | Write "Thank You" letter. Follow up with referrals. |

*Key points:*

Software industry booming. Lots of opportunities for engineering types.
Impressed with quality assurance experience. Liked broad range of skills/especially project and people management.
Geophysics background not pertinent.

*Suggestions:*

Gave the following referrals:
John Smith, Softtime, Inc., phone no.
Eileen Brown, Multi-Media Gulch, phone no.

Brainstorming ideas with people you respect is one of the benefits of networking. They can provide you with important feedback and additional information that may be critical to your final decision. Do not be afraid to discard ideas that do not seem realistic or workable, but be careful not to throw them away too soon.

When Jay was investigating the managed health care industry, he spoke with twenty-eight people in various companies. During these informational interviews he realized that the managed health care field was not right for him. "I can't tell you how disappointed I was. I spoke with a lot of people, and I did not connect with many on a professional or personal level. Overall they were not impressed or excited by my skills and experience. I intuitively knew I had to give it up and look somewhere else." That was the lowest point of the entire process for him, but once he realized his original path was not going anywhere, he set out in another direction.

### *Deal Realistically with Financial Constraints*

Earlier in this book we suggested that you review your personal budget. Concerns about money are real and influence many decisions, but you do not want these fears to control your life. Instead, look carefully again at how you are spending your money and try to find additional areas where you can economize even if you are employed. The more financial flexibility you can give yourself, the more ability you have to look for the right position or project.

Jay says it is important not to give up everything. He and his wife had two teenagers, a mortgage, and responsibility for aging parents. They were understandably nervous and frightened as their savings declined, but they were determined to maintain their social life as individuals and as a couple. They felt it was important not to become hermits during this period. Socializing with their friends gave them stability and emotional support.

If you are not used to thinking about how you spend your money, this period will be difficult for you. Jeanie felt one of her biggest hurdles was having to forego personal luxuries. She had to force herself to go out with people even though she did not have a new outfit or could not afford to eat at the newest restaurants. But in the end she felt good about being able to stay within her budget.

Other people, like Jay and his wife, have serious financial obligations like mortgages, loans, or college tuition. If you fall into this group, you may have to find temporary sources of income or remain in your current position until you find something else.

### *Take on Project Work*

Being able to earn income, add to your Portfolio of Assets, widen your network, and demonstrate your value in the marketplace makes taking on project work or volunteering for special projects an appealing alternative while you are researching new markets. Ideally these projects will be in areas you are considering as future directions. Realistically, though, it may be easier to find projects in your current industry or area of expertise. There are many sources for project work. You are likely to find out about them from the people you talk with during your networking. Specialized agencies, which place managers in interim projects and specific jobs, have grown rapidly. Volunteering may lead to paid projects and offers opportunities to broaden your skill base and make important connections.

Often, it makes sense to pursue several paths simultaneously, as Tom did. He was a civil engineer whose dream was to be a consultant and live in the Middle East. But, with all the unrest in that part of the world, he questioned whether the timing was right. So he sought other options including some domestic, short-term engineering projects. By working on a number of different projects, he was able to make new connections and diversify his Portfolio of Assets. Through one of the projects, he created a position for himself in an organization that managed contracts in Saudi Arabia.

Some of our clients take on project work out of financial necessity and find that they enjoy it as a permanent way of life. Others use project work as a way to get into a company, meet people, and land a full-time position. Internal Free Agents use special projects to gain additional visibility and skills. Regardless of your situation, project work offers many benefits as long as you choose projects carefully and continue researching markets. If you let up on your Positioning activities, you will have nothing to fall back on when the project is completed. Even though it is hard to find time to research markets and to network while you are working, schedule these activities into your daily and weekly plan.

### *Be Persistent*

Sometimes it is difficult to avoid feeling dejected or discouraged. But you need to be persistent in this stage, even if you feel like giving up.

As one client says, "Don't let the no's get you down." Jay found that he got a lot of "thanks, but no thanks" from people as he was networking. He wanted to be direct and confident but not pushy. He decided to let people know that he was interested and motivated, and had valuable skills to offer. He was tenacious but not obnoxious, and when he heard no a second time, he graciously thanked the person and went on to the next contact. His advice about being persistent: talk to a lot of people, make sure there is a demand for your skills, and know when to politely back away.

## Making Your Decision

Collecting information about markets can become a full-time occupation. Once you begin talking with people about their needs, the process becomes fun and exciting. But at some point you need to make a decision about what market or markets you are going to pursue. As you make your decision, the key factors to consider are market fit, your degree of passion for the work, and the possibilities for establishing credibility in the field.

*Market fit.* Identify which market needs you can meet with your current Portfolio of Assets. Where can you best leverage your skills? Jay was excited when telecommunications began making sense: he fit well with the people, the business, and the products. The telecommunications industry needed creative deal makers like him. His project-management skills were an asset in the fast-paced environment. He was convinced that there were good opportunities for someone with his background.

*Passion.* Determine which market you are excited about. Which aspects of a market interest you? You have an opportunity to choose markets and customers that are stimulating or new. In addition to fitting into the market, Jay found that he was excited about the telecommunications industry. The more he delved into it, the more people he talked to, the more pleased he became. He found the people so involved with their products and their organizations that it was contagious. He felt more energetic than he had in years.

When he was offered his current position, he could not believe that he would be paid for doing work that seemed so enjoyable.

*Credibility.* Consider the perceptions that customers have of you and your Portfolio of Assets. You want to choose markets where you can quickly establish your credibility and expertise. Jeanie realized that although she had the skills to design her new products, she did not have experience to bring them to market. While putting together her business plan, Jeanie realized how much trouble she was going to have breaking out of her narrow slot and gaining credibility. She had to fill in the gaps before she could launch her own products. As a first step she joined a team charged with designing and launching a new consumer product over the next eight months. She profited from people's willingness to help her acquire the marketing and financial knowledge that she was lacking and that she needed to be credible.

As you are deciding what direction you want to follow, you may find that you need some additional information. Most likely you will also want to talk through your ideas with your coach, buddy, or someone particularly knowledgeable about your potential choice. Connecting disparate information will lead to new ideas. Identifying key issues, reframing the problem, and coming up with new conclusions will help you make a good decision.

Tony was at a dead end in trying to figure out how to combine what appeared to be unconnected skills and interests: Peace Corps, retail consulting, language fluency, travel, and public relations. As he spoke with people in his network he learned that the large consulting companies wanted to set up retail consulting practices in Eastern Europe. He realized he could be the perfect candidate for a consultant position.

## Making the Sale

When I interview prospective candidates, I want them to tell me how valuable they will be to me and my organization. I want to hear less about the responsibilities they had in their previous position

> and more about how they will use their skills for me. I am looking for accomplishments and value.

Once you identify the markets you want to pursue, you will need to begin selling yourself as a Free Agent—that is, strongly stating your value to prospective customers. A Silicon Valley CEO tells the following cautionary tale:

> The other day I interviewed a man who had been downsized. I asked, "What have you done?" He answered, "For the last fifteen years, I was the manager of a product-processing department." I asked, "Well, what did you do?" "We processed the new product, particularly on the administration side." I said, "Yes, and what did you exactly do?" "Well, I was the manager of the department." "Oh, and what did the department look like?" "I had twelve people who reported to me, and we processed these new products." We had an entire conversation in which he conveyed little information. He was unable to communicate his skills in a way that demonstrated to me how he could create value for me and my organization.

Contrast this applicant with Angela, who decided she wanted to be the vice president of sales in her company.

> I went in for the interview and was told that there were five other candidates and that each of them did something better than I did. Since I knew all of them, I just went down the line and said, "Look, if you want to concentrate on short-term profits, Joe is your man. If shaping up the sales team to get better results is your goal, Bill is the one. If you want to notch up overseas sales, take Marge." And so on down the list. And then I said, "But I can do all of those things plus this, this, and this. I am the only one who can do them all, and I think you want them all done in a reasonable time frame." I was not exaggerating, I knew I could deliver.

Her knowledge of her competition, her directness, and her ability to describe how she would use her skills to meet the company's needs were important in getting the position.

Here are some other pointers for Positioning:

- Know the company.
- Know the competition.
- Know your Portfolio of Assets.
- Identify the customer's needs.
- Describe your accomplishments in terms of their needs.
- Explain how your skills meet customer needs.
- Express strong interest and excitement; be energetic.
- Ask for the job!

When answering questions about yourself, remember that you are always selling your Portfolio of Assets. Talk about past positions and projects, and focus on accomplishments and results. If you show how your accomplishments are transferable and will meet needs and create value in an organization, you will come across as assured and knowledgeable. If you believe in yourself and your potential, others will also.

As you repackage and present yourself in a new and attractive way remember to emphasize:

- Your strongest skills and abilities. "I'm skilled at forming alliances and persuading those for whom I don't have formal responsibility to follow through."
- Your greatest accomplishments. "The value I added was. . . ."
- Your ability to apply your skills and expertise (how will you add value?). "From what we've just discussed, I can see how my understanding of the psychology of your customers and products will enable all of us to hit our targets."
- Your ability to fulfill your goals. "I want to leverage my strong skills in a company with dominant market share and new products in the pipeline. You fit that profile for me."

Being a Free Agent means always Positioning yourself in order to find markets and projects. Even when you are working on a project or hold the position of your dreams, continue looking for new and emerging applications for your skills.

In Part One of this book we have provided a process for becoming a Free Agent. We have discussed in detail the first three stages. As individuals become Free Agents, they adopt new expectations for their workplace. So, in Part Two we look at what organizations are experiencing as they try to create environments to which Free Agents want to come and in which they want to do their best work. In our research we found an interesting phenomenon: as more individuals are becoming Free Agents, more companies are using the same process for becoming Free Agent communities. The next four chapters explore this thesis in detail.

Part Two

# *Becoming a Free Agent Community*

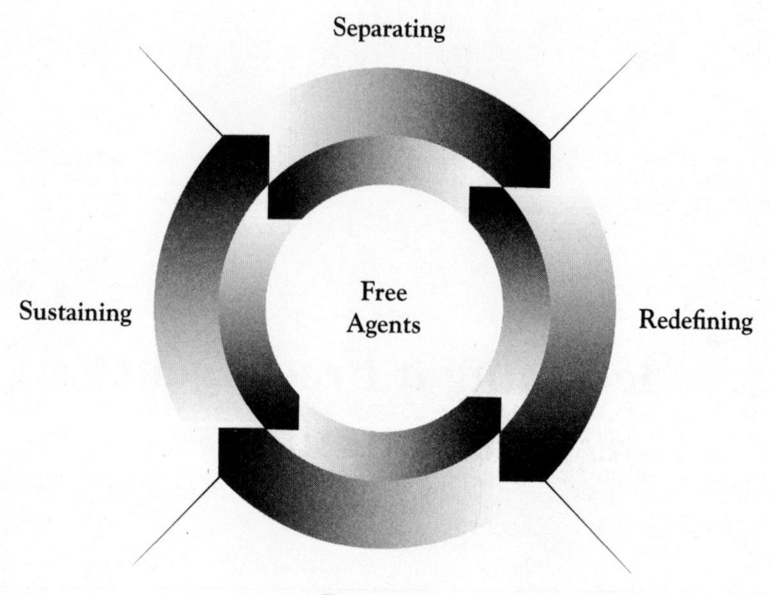
Separating
Free
Agents
Sustaining
Redefining
Positioning

*Chapter Six*

# The Need for Corporate Change

## Sailing into Uncharted Waters

> The only certainty is that . . . breakpoint change will occur and will do so on a regular basis. In such a world, a central task for the leadership of any organization is to help individuals and the organization as a whole come to grips with the reality of a future that can only be partially foreseen, if it is foreseeable at all.
>
> —*J. H. Boyett and J. T. Boyett,* Beyond Workplace 2000

When Tanya began what turned out to be a twenty-year career with one organization, she was happy just to have a job with a solid company. Over the years she realized that she had acquired valuable skills, and gradually she became a Free Agent. She had no thought of leaving the company. She enjoyed her work and her colleagues. She frequently rotated jobs, was able to work independently, and was continuously adding skills. Most important, she believed in the company and its values. However, when competition increased, new managers were brought in who had different expectations and treated people poorly. Tanya no longer liked the way the business was run, and she felt the corporation was no longer a congenial place for employees like her. Once she realized she could not work well in the new environment, she found new markets for her skills, experience, and knowledge.

So far in this book we have been looking at how people can take charge and become Free Agents. In our consulting business and throughout our interviews, we discerned a factor beyond those we have already discussed that is central to Free Agents' success: their relationship to their workplace. As people become Free Agents, this relationship changes because they recognize and accept that corporate care and longevity are no longer a reality or a necessity. Contrasted with non-Free Agents, who continue to want and need corporations to take care of them, Free Agents seek a more equal relationship. They want greater control over how they do their work, where they work, and for how long. They are searching for places where their contributions will accrue to both the company and to themselves. "They . . . seek to excel, not out of a sense of fear or obligation but because they truly enjoy contributing to their own success, the success of their peers and the success of the community at large" (James, 1996, p. 68).

Free Agents want an environment where they can work together with others to produce something of value. They understand that on their own they cannot convert their skills into products and services. They need organizations to provide the ongoing platform and resources so that they can produce their best work and continue to learn (Drucker, 1994, p. 68). And they want to be part of a community where they can "function with a collective energy even greater than the sum of their individual energies" (Zemke, 1996, p. 27). They are asking companies to provide them with a community of interdependent individuals who participate together in discussion and decision making, and who share common practices that both nurture and define the community (Bellah and others, 1985, p. 333).

Companies that understand this new relationship and are taking the steps to strengthen it are in the lead in gaining competitive advantage. In this new symbiotic relationship both parties are once again meeting their needs; there is a union between the new worker and the new ways of doing business. Employees and employers have a rare opportunity to transform the workplace into a new kind of community where "the company offers [employees] not permanent employment, but challenges that give them an opportunity to develop their interests, and a promise of mutual dialogue and openness. . . . Employees become dedicated to accomplishing the current mission, working with others who are similarly dedicated. They offer not obedience, but intelligence: they will not do whatever they are asked, but they *will* do whatever they can to further the mission. The relationship lasts as long as the organizational vision and the individual commitments are close enough to lead to a sense of mutual contribution" (Heckscher, 1995, pp. 145–146).

## The New Community

> Companies have always understood that customers are volunteers. We need to see that employees, too, are volunteers. They have options. If we're going to persuade the best people to choose us and to stay with us, we must develop a new kind of work environment [Haas, 1993, p. 105].

As Drucker explains, "The old communities—family, village, parish, and so on—have all but disappeared in the knowledge society. Their place has largely been taken by the new unit of social integration, the organization. Where community was fate, organization is voluntary membership" (1994, p. 72). This notion of voluntary membership is at the heart of the new relationship Free Agents are defining with their organizations.

As individuals fine-tune their skills and increase their value in the marketplace, they are much less likely than they were previously to accept compromises in their work situations. They are aware of the importance of finding environments where they can produce high-quality work and enjoy personal and professional freedom. And they can afford to be choosy. With increased mobility and opportunities, Free Agents can now choose which organization they will work for, where in the organization they will be, which role(s) they will play, and how long they will stay.

Free Agents repeatedly tell us that whether they sense a common purpose with a company strongly influences their decision to commit to or disengage from it. They want to feel that they are contributing members of a larger team that is making a difference. In these companies, "community is like a crisp salad in which all the ingredients (in this case, people) retain their individuality, yet make something greater than the sum of the parts" (Gozdz, 1993, p. 108). In the old corporate environment, which was defined by security and stability, community existed as a result of longevity. The workplace became a community because the same people tended to work together under one roof for their entire careers.

This is not true in an organization that values performance and contribution above loyalty and seniority. In a rapidly changing business environment, where people come and go based on their skills and business needs, community does not just happen automatically. The real challenge for organizations today is to transform a collection of individuals into a nurturing and ongoing community based on a mature relationship between employer and employee rather than the parent-child relationship of the past. In some organizations senior management is driving this transition. In other companies only isolated mid-level managers and team leaders have begun the transition.

As we saw in Part One, individual Free Agents need to adopt new attitudes and behaviors. Organizations and their managers also need to make the same kinds of shifts. Organizations that do not will have difficulties persuading their employees to put the welfare of the company ahead of their personal gains. An absence of trust often negatively affects productivity and results.

Companies and teams within organizations that are successfully forming Free Agent communities recognize that they must translate Free Agents' needs and expectations into corporate initiatives. Free Agents' needs and expectations include:

- Clear corporate direction
- Two-way, honest, and open communication
- Access to financial and strategic information
- Shared decision making

- Quick and effective feedback
- Recognition from peers and senior management
- A sense of achievement
- Challenges and interesting work
- Resources to do the job
- Opportunities for career development, skill enhancement, and self-renewal
- Ability to work autonomously

The corporate initiatives that fulfill these needs are

- Clear and operational corporate vision
- Enhanced communication and information sharing
- Compensation and reward systems that focus on individual and team performance
- Recruiting and hiring practices that clearly define skills needed and involve the whole team
- Frequent and effective performance evaluation
- Continuous learning opportunities

For example, Free Agents need access to information that affects their ability to do their jobs. In response, some companies are sharing financial and strategic information that was once reserved only for senior management. Likewise, Free Agents want to be recognized for both their individual successes and their team contributions. Companies recognize this need by revamping their compensation systems. They are devising ways to reward front-line employees for their skills, knowledge, and the overall performance of their business unit. In this way, management can reward outstanding individual and team achievement.

In the remaining chapters in Part Two we will share the new approaches some companies and teams are taking in these areas as they attempt to build a solid foundation for a viable, ongoing Free Agent community.

## The Process of Building Community

In Part One we described the process that individuals go through as they become Free Agents. As we interviewed professionals who are attempting to re-create a sense of community in their organizations, we realized that organizations undergo a similar transition process. However, although the process is analogous, the work that organizations do in each stage is different. As organizations undertake change their managers need to Separate from old beliefs and practices, Redefine their corporate systems to meet Free Agents' needs and to support and motivate their Free Agents, Position themselves in the marketplace to attract Free Agents, and Sustain a complex and decentralized community. Although the model at the beginning of this chapter looks familiar, the terms are used here in reference to organizations rather than to individuals.

The individuals we interviewed were surprisingly consistent in their descriptions of each stage of the process. These stages are previewed below and are explored more completely in subsequent chapters. Although we depict the process as circular, it does not move in a single direction. Steps sometimes have to be retraced; the process sometimes stops completely for a while.

During the Separating stage, managers discard old tenets and practices as they begin to take themselves and the company in new directions. Senior management commits to creating a new type of community and develops and articulates a clear vision and value system for the organization.

During the Redefining stage management develops the infrastructure that enables Free Agents to make their best contributions to the company. Managers redesign and rebuild the company's communication and information-sharing, compensation, recognition, and performance-management systems.

During the Positioning stage, management formulates and initiates strategies for competing for skills in a competitive marketplace and for developing Free Agents. Managers analyze and make necessary changes in their recruiting and hiring practices and in the career-development opportunities they provide.

During the Sustaining stage, management develops and implements strategies for supporting a dynamic and fluid Free Agent community. Managers may also develop techniques for including off-site employees, consultants, freelancers, and contingency workers as part of this Free Agent community.

## Challenges

Competition is creating a constant need to improve performance and hasten product development. Businesses are often forced to do more with less, offer fewer career and advancement opportunities, and increase managers' spans of control. They are faced with the pressing need for value creators and the ability to configure flexible, skilled teams speedily. Their workforce may not have the skills that match new business requirements.

How do companies respond to these challenges? They must help their current people become Free Agents, and they must be seen as desirable employers. They must make the systemic changes that will attract other Free Agents and sustain an ongoing community.

As organizations begin to make these changes, friction may occur. Sometimes managers and corporations push individuals to change quickly, but most often individuals outpace their organizations. In a sense this situation is not surprising. Although individuals may resist change, they also have the capacity to adapt faster than organizations, which have to make structural changes—a feat that is never easy.

Some companies and managers have begun this process. Others are stymied by their inability to acknowledge the need to change or to initiate the change itself. As Professor Prahalad of the University of Michigan explains it, "You are telling top management that their accumulated intellectual capital is devalued, that their 30 years of personal experience is less valuable as we move forward. This is so traumatic that senior managers find it hard to change unless there's a crisis" (quoted in Sherman, 1993, p. 51).

Acknowledging the need to change is the necessary first step for managers. Many have not realized or are unwilling to admit that the new workforce has different values and priorities. When managers are unable to understand these changes, companies experience several kinds of problems: they are unable to hire and retain committed people with the necessary skills, to maximize the effectiveness of the workforce, and to persuade their non-Free Agent workforce to change.

Most organizations do not change until managers can no longer ignore the problems they are having. A production manager at a manufacturing company shared a lament that we heard many times. "I had a wonderful person who knew our operating system better than anyone. I depended on her troubleshooting skills; I knew she would always come through for me. You know what happened? She told me she needed more flexibility in her schedule. Would you believe, I tied my own hands. I refused because I was afraid that everyone else in the group would want the same thing. She left. I can see now that if I don't change my thinking, I'll lose more key people."

Making the change, which is the second step required to create a Free Agent community, involves the willingness to live with uncertainty and loss of control. Some farsighted managers are willing to accept these conditions and to take the actions necessary to begin the process. They replace traditional systems with new ones that meet workers' expectations. They focus on controlling the work rather than the people. They are coaches rather than watchdogs. They provide their Free Agents with critical information and feedback and run interference for them in the organization. Most of all, they enable and allow their Free Agents to work autonomously (Haas, 1993, p. 105).

In addition, these corporations and their managers are able to reduce short-term profits in order to realize long-term gains. Building a community takes time. It is not a quick fix. When companies do not see results immediately, they tend to change course and thus never realize the benefits of investing time and money in their human assets and of changing their organizations' infrastructure. Creating and sustaining a Free Agent community is an ongoing commitment.

## Accepting the Challenge

> Information Age management means relinquishing old ideas of hierarchical command and control in favor of a new cultural paradigm that embraces the individual [James, 1996, p. 63].

Some managers may ask whether the idea of a Free Agent community is not just another fad. People we spoke to in organizations do not think so. In fact, they strongly believe that having Free Agents is a key competitive strategy for the future. If indeed the workforce is changing profoundly, creating environments that can harness the potential of these new workers is not a fad.

One CEO told us that "companies that do not meet expectations lose people, and often they are good people. I don't think Free Agents are harder to please, but they do have different goals. They're just more hawkish about their timetable and the quality of their experience. I think as a manager you have to accept this as reality and make the appropriate changes."

The remainder of Part Two is devoted to exploring the new ways in which some companies are building communities for Free Agents. As with anything new, many of the systems described are far from definitive. But even though the number of companies attempting to create Free Agent communities is growing steadily, managers may not know what others are doing in this arena. Therefore, our intent here is to provide change agents with initial ideas for designing dynamic companies that will succeed in attracting Free Agents in an increasingly competitive marketplace.

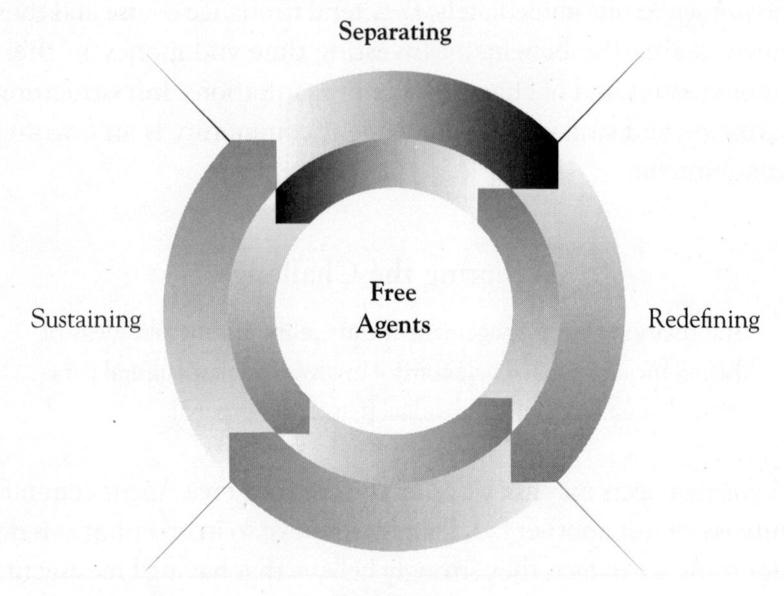
Separating
Free
Agents
Sustaining
Redefining
Positioning

*Chapter Seven*

# Corporate Separating

## Embracing the New

> The new leader is a motivator, coordinator, and diplomat, as opposed to a controller, autocrat, and dispenser of discipline. The power and authority of these new leaders will come from their own knowledge, abilities, and influence—not from the positions they hold or the size of their organization.
>
> —L. D. Runge, *"The Manager and the Information Worker of the 1990s"*

Ellen is CEO of a mid-size software company. She started her business ten years ago with one very popular product, a software developer, and an office assistant. Today, her company has over a hundred employees, many additions to the product line, and soaring profits. Ellen realized early on that being successful demanded a cadre of highly skilled employees with a Free Agent philosophy. In order to entice these individuals and harness their creativity, she had to meet their needs and align their interests with those of her company. She had to let go of preconceived ideas about the way companies were supposed to be managed. She had to find some new strategies that would work.

Mike is CEO of a company that manufactures medical devices. Over the company's twenty-five year history, it has experienced many different leadership styles, slowly evolving from a bureaucratic hierarchy to a Free Agent community. In the seven years since Mike arrived, he has driven major changes throughout the organization. From the start, he knew his management team would have to alter its ways in order to attract and keep the new breed of workers. Now there is much more participatory decision making throughout the company. Employees at all levels are provided the information and latitude they need to make informed decisions. Individuals are recognized for their skills, knowledge, and contributions rather than for their longevity. The days of closed-door, top-down management are long gone.

Mike explains that he had these management ideas many years ago, but he was not able to articulate them clearly. They ran totally counter to the accepted wisdom of the time. Being ahead of his peers got him into trouble. Now he is convinced that his success in creating a community for skilled, productive individuals justifies the dramatic changes he pioneered.

These CEOs are attempting to create an environment that meets Free Agents' needs for clear direction and boundaries, autonomy, access to information, and participation in decision making. They both have found that in order to achieve this goal their managers have had to detach themselves from timeworn ways of operating businesses and managing individuals. This shedding process, so aptly described by Ellen and Mike, is called *Separating*. The Separating stage provides an opportunity for managers to realize new directions for themselves as well as for their companies.

Earlier in the book we explained that Separating for individuals is characterized by endings and beginnings. For organizations, Separating is similar. As managers relinquish old roles, they can accept and implement new ways of providing Free Agents with the tools, information, and support they need to produce their best work. This stage also provides the opportunity for the company to begin clarifying its vision and values.

Separating is no easier for companies than it is for individuals. Although some managers find that this stage validates practices they are already committed to, many others find this stage troublesome because it requires them to change in basic ways. Mike recalls that one of his most significant activities during his first year was working with his management team to develop a vision for the company. A main thrust of the vision was to provide better customer service than the competition. The highest priorities were to hire and retain customer-focused individuals, to invest in developing them, and to provide them with the best technology available. Mike wanted his customer-service people to have the ability to provide solutions as problems arose.

Mike had complete confidence in the company's new vision and goals, but getting the support of the managers who worked for him was another story. For the company to succeed, all managers had to support this vision enthusiastically and impart it to their employees. Like many individuals, some of the them wanted to keep the status quo, which had demanded less accountability and had worked well for them in the past. They were afraid of the new expectations implied in this vision. It meant they would have to transfer power, share expertise, and coach their people much more than in the past. The new vision represented a departure from their usual style. They had to be convinced to take the risk to change their behaviors so that they could make the vision real to others.

## Getting on Board

> Managers who are responsible for the transformation never say, "This is the way we've done it for twenty years" or even "This is the way we've done it for five years." Like people in a boat swept along in a fast-moving river, they don't complain that the current is moving; they knew it was when they got on board.

Managers we talked with echoed Mike. Change is never easy. Here are the major shifts managers who are committed to creating a Free Agent community will need to make:

| *From* | *To* |
|---|---|
| Believing that the company vision is a static statement | Believing that the company vision is the driver of culture, strategy, and tactics |

| *From* | *To* |
|---|---|
| Closely guarding information | Instantaneously providing unfiltered information |
| Practicing top-down decision making | Practicing participatory decision making |
| Creating hierarchical, multilevel organizations | Creating flattened, networked organizations |
| Stressing rules and procedures | Stressing results and outcomes |
| Basing compensation on longevity | Basing compensation on skills, knowledge, and contributions |
| Treating employees as interchangeable commodities | Treating employees as assets |
| Acknowledging leadership and power derived from position | Acknowledging leadership derived from skill and knowledge |
| Granting narrow responsibility, limited to a specific job | Granting broad responsibility, not bound by a job description |

In a company where these new beliefs prevail, all employees are clear about what the organization expects, values, and gives in return for their hard work. Mike makes sure that everyone in the company hears the same message. "We are not looking for long-term, loyal employees but for individuals with the right skill sets and the ability to contribute to the company's success. Our responsibility to these people is to give them the best possible place to work and the freedom and tools to get the job done."

In the best of all worlds, the process of Separating would begin at the top of an organization and trickle down. But because making companywide changes can be so difficult, in reality Separating occurs at many levels in organizations. Kim-Lei, a controller, decided that if she waited for her company to change, she would probably lose all her talented Free Agents. She knew that she needed to do things differently with her group. She cut through company policies wherever possible so that she could act as a facilitator and not as a boss. Other managers in the company viewed Kim-Lei's group as an anomaly and never did understand why it was doing so well.

The Separating process presents new demands and expectations. Leaders who are able to meet these challenges become the models for managing Free Agents and creating a new type of community. They have to change their customary ways of operating in three areas: they have to articulate clearly the purpose of the organization; they have to communicate openly; and they have to relinquish tight management controls.

## Clarity of Purpose

> I think front-line people always question why management is doing what we're doing. The more they understand about our vision and our mission and the more we are consistent in our actions, the more we can expect from our employees. Everything we do is aligned with our values and mission statement.

Free Agents are attracted to companies with an overriding purpose and clear direction. They search for organizations that are explicit about how they deal with their community, their individual employees, and their customers. Because Free Agents are asked to work together as a team to achieve common goals, they need the map that a clearly articulated vision provides. A vision statement describes the company's culture and expectations and provides the basis for making decisions and for developing and implementing control systems. It explicitly explains the reason for the company's existence. As Collins and Porras explain in *Built to Last: Successful Habits of Visionary Companies*, "Like the fundamental ideals of a great nation, church, school or any other enduring institution, core ideology in a visionary company is a set of basic precepts that plant a fixed stake in the ground. 'This is who we are; this is what we stand for; this is what we're all about'" (1994, p. 54).

Vision is certainly not a new concept. Business gurus over the past several decades have been telling us about its importance and value. But in many companies vision is overstated and underutilized. Management teams spend long hours developing a vision and turning it into a mission statement that is often too cumbersome or too vague to be useful. Such statements are not integrated into the fiber of the business; they never become operational and eventually are considered irrelevant (Kotter, 1995, p. 63).

Mike says that his company's vision statement was ignored before he arrived. Employees felt let down by management's lack of mission and sense of urgency. Salespeople never thought about their company's vision, even though they needed it the most. When they were poised to make critical promises to a customer, they needed to understand exactly how the company expected them to do business. They needed the leadership to be as customer-focused as they were. But once they made the sale, no one else kept the commitments they made to their customers. Fulfillment was a nightmare. As a result, the sales department was always at war with manufacturing. And ultimately the customer lost.

In some companies, however, managers have shifted from seeing vision as a static statement to viewing it as the driver of their culture, strategy, and tactics. They acknowledge that the corporate vision statement is no longer a nice-to-have but a need-to-have. For everyone in the company it provides consistent answers to these critical questions: What do we believe in? How do we operate as a company? How do we conduct business? Why are we all here?

Specifically, a vision statement does the following:

- Highlights the company's competitive advantage
- Defines the business
- Defines company values and purpose—what the company stands for
- Defines boundaries for decision making and behavior

- Sets expectations for how things are done within the company
- Describes the work environment
- Inspires employees even in hard times

An organization's vision can be expressed in different ways. It can be a set of detailed statements or just a brief paragraph. Vision statements are sometimes called principles or core values. But form and terminology are not nearly as important as commitment to the statement at the highest level, wide dissemination, and constant reinforcement (Kotter, 1995, p. 64).

Here are two examples of vision statements:

> Our Vision: Compaq, along with our partners, will deliver compelling products and services of the highest quality that will transform computing into an intuitive experience that extends human capability on all planes—communication, education, work, and play [Compaq Computer, 1996, p. 22].

> Our Mission: The mission of Bristol-Myers Squibb is to extend and enhance human life by providing the highest quality health and personal care products. Our aim is to be the preeminent global diversified health and personal care company. We have three priorities: growth, productivity and a dynamic operating culture [Bristol-Myers Squibb Company, 1996, p. 5].

Mike recalls that when his management team was developing a vision, he did some research to identify the "right" set of core values for his company. He found that there was no such thing. The statement simply had to capture what the company stood for and how it would define success over the long term. Mike and his senior staff took a hard look at their beliefs and values and at how they could meet the needs of their new workforce. Those became the "right" principles for them. Mike says that the key indicators of the success of the statement are how deeply everyone in the organization believes in the vision and how consistently they express it in everything they do.

In companies where the CEO and the senior management team make the vision operational, managers and their employees use it to

- Establish business objectives and measure progress
- Provide strategic direction for all employees
- Set project goals and objectives
- Articulate boundaries for decision making
- Develop compensation and reward systems
- Direct recruiting and hiring efforts
- Evaluate individual performance and drive skill development
- Provide a dispersed workforce with a sense of belonging and of sharing a common purpose with headquarters
- Provide a consistent message to customers

Because Mike and his managers want to hire a diverse workforce whose values are congruent with those of the company, everyone has to be able to communicate the company's values when they are recruiting and hiring. All of the company's new employees, contractors, and consultants have to understand how the company does business. "Honesty, integrity, urgency, customer and shareholder trust guide everything we do here. Once people understand what we stand for, they are able to decide whether their personal values are matched with ours. When they are, that seamless alignment works."

Luckily, Ellen has always been a stickler about clarifying and communicating the company's direction and values. Her people tell her how unusual it is for a company to have such a sense of purpose. By adhering to it, they can feel confident of their decision-making abilities and are likely to make sound choices. Ellen is convinced that vision creates and sustains community and produces the results she desires. She sees it as the bedrock of her company's culture.

## Communication

> Information is, I believe, a most undervalued commodity. There is power in knowing something someone else doesn't, which explains why executives are so often loath to share information with employees [Semler, 1993, p. 286].

If withholding information is personal power, then sharing information is collective gain. Free Agents need and expect clear and open communication in their work environment. They understand that information is a critical tool for making timely decisions, being productive, and providing value to an organization. They tend to be attracted to companies that share information widely and instantaneously. They consciously look for communities where managers disseminate information rather than guard and keep it.

Traditionally senior management limited the amount and type of information communicated throughout an organization. Because senior managers were responsible for making most of the decisions, they believed that only they needed access to certain business and financial data. Even when they shared information more broadly, it was filtered through multiple managerial levels.

When communication channels are narrow, people often feel dependent and insecure. They spend a great deal of time and energy fueling highly active rumor mills, which are often based on misinterpretations and inaccuracies. As one manager explains, "It was like running a race with one of your legs tied to the other one. How could I do my best when I did not have the tools I needed? The only people with power and the ability to achieve results were those with the information."

Freeing up communication is an essential step in creating a Free Agent community. The more access to information people throughout the organization have, the more effective they can be. Managers need to overcome fears that prevent them from sharing information. Some of the most common barriers to open communication are: belief that a manager's primary role is to screen information and make decisions unilaterally, fear of losing power and control, fear of no longer having a role in the organization, and fear that information will be shared with competitors.

In the Separating stage, managers struggle to let go of these inhibitors so they can move on to more effective practices. One manager changed when she understood that if she wanted her team members to have a strong reputation internally and to be viewed as business experts, she needed to provide them with a broad base of information. She and her people had to understand the big picture, not just their field of technical expertise. In *Open-Book Management: The Coming Business Revolution*, John Case advises managers to "get the information out there! Tell employees not only what they need to know to do their jobs effectively, but how the division or the company as a whole is doing" (1995, p. 61). As one manager summed it up, "When people have a great deal of information, it is a different game. They can do what you hired them to do."

Managers who are committed to sharing information no longer wait for information to pass through the old hierarchical levels. They are proactive and aggressive in acquiring and communicating information. These managers become good listeners and champion two-way communication with their teams, peers, and others with whom they work (Haas, 1993, p. 106).

Mike tells us that he expects his project leaders to provide their teams with all the pertinent data available. He knows it is no longer enough to say, "We'll just do it because that's what needs to get done." In large, complex organizations, a lot gets done just "because." In his organization a lot gets done because individuals have made informed decisions that are good for business.

Open communication is not a new concept. In 1954, Drucker wrote that an employee "should be enabled to control, measure and guide his own performance" (p. 306). He advised managers that employees need to understand how their "work relates to the work of the whole" (p. 307). He believed that information was a key to motivating employees to improve their performance (p. 307). He might as well have been talking about meeting the needs of Free Agents.

Drucker realized that new tools were needed to get this information out to people quickly. Now the technology exists. Even though the amount of information increases daily, with new technology companies can share this information electronically with all levels simultaneously and rapidly. Mike does not want his people to have to wait to hear about a new corporate direction or a rationale for a difficult decision. He estimates that it takes about three weeks to get information through a hierarchy and that all who receive information in this way interpret it and pass it on differently. Today with e-mail and a dedicated communications hotline his employees get strategic information on a daily basis.

What types of information should be shared? Confidentiality is often a consideration along with concerns about proprietary information. Ellen tells us that her management team is not overly concerned about information leaking; they figure the competition is too busy worrying about themselves. Case recommends sharing the company's "pivotal operational numbers": income statements, cash-flow statements, and balance sheets (1995, p. 66). Mike's philosophy is that all of the company's information except personnel files and compensation information should be available to everyone because he wants all employees to be involved in increasing degrees in developing budgets and plans. Throughout the year, managers gather small groups to assess company progress against projections, refine objectives, and discuss new options. In general, managers who believe in the importance of sharing information find few barriers that cannot be overcome.

## Control

> A manager is not unlike a captain of a ship. The captain's job is to guide the ship to its destination. . . . [Captains] cannot do this if they are down in the hold, tying knots and securing the cargo [Runge, 1994, p. 9].

Free Agents look for environments where they have the freedom to do their work. They find it difficult to operate effectively with tight management controls. Historically, organizational control was top-down. Management prescribed the boundaries with little input from the troops and then monitored and enforced those boundaries. This paternalistic and highly structured environment often diminished individuals' sense of self-worth and prevented people from solving problems, making decisions, and contributing effectively to the bottom line. In addition, these controls tended to discourage creativity, resourcefulness, and agility.

Rather than strict, confining controls, Free Agents need broad limits within which to use their talents and exercise their creativity. Simple guidelines for performance enable them to move in the same direction as the organization. Mike views controls as a map; they indicate the destination for his Free Agents, but they do not prescribe the route. He intentionally leaves it up to the managers and individuals to determine their own course, while company policies outline the rules, the expectations, and acceptable actions. In order to create this type of environment, management needs to replace ineffective attitudes about control and command with new ones that provide direction and order and get people invested in the company and in the community.

Managers admit that this part of Separating is frightening. The fear of losing power and of not obtaining desired results presents a hurdle in this stage. Many managers automatically take charge when crises arise. They rush in and fix the problems themselves. But Free Agents are not accustomed to having people step in and take over. They are confident of their ability to handle problems and tough situations. The challenge for managers is to remain on the sidelines, run interference inside and outside the company, and provide support and direction (Stewart, 1994, p. 50). Coming from a pyramidal environment, even Mike finds it difficult to resist taking control. To his credit, he knows that if he tries to play the hero, he will quickly undermine the new management style he has introduced.

Another deep-rooted fear is that of expendability. If managers relinquish control will the organization still need them? What are the benefits of giving up traditional control? Managers who are successfully making the transition to a new approach are learning a new role and beginning to feel comfortable with it. When they cease micromanaging, they are freed to become teachers and coordinators. They are involved in new activities such as: developing strategies and tactics that are aligned with the corporate vision; setting clear goals and objectives; providing their teams with needed information, resources, and support; defining checkpoints and benchmarks for performance; and participating in higher-level decision making and problem solving (Simons, 1995, p. 88). By sharing control managers are able to help individuals become and remain Free Agents, navigate change, and remain inspired and motivated during rough times (Jaffe, Scott, and Tobe, 1994, pp. 207–208).

Mike believes that hands-on supervision creates unnecessary overhead because two people are doing the job of one. He wants managers to see themselves as coaches. He expects them to hire people with the skills they need and to ensure that new employees receive appropriate training and support so the managers can spend their time building community and expanding their own skill sets.

## Creating an Oasis

My biggest obstacles are other managers and the person I report to. They complain that I am giving my team too much authority and autonomy. They still think managing is about controlling. They

> hire and retain people with different attitudes from those of my group, which makes working with them difficult. My team is not aligned with the rest of the organization.

Ideally, an entire organization should be able to experience Separating at the same time, but this is not always possible. Because individuals often go through this process more quickly than organizations, individual managers like Kim-Lei may adopt a new approach before the entire company does.

These managers are creating pockets of Free Agent communities in spite of the fact that their organizations do not encourage, reinforce, or recognize their efforts. Such managers successfully nurture an environment for Free Agents. Even though the systems of the organization do not support their management philosophy and actions, they succeed at protecting their groups and creating a strong sense of community.

Carlos sees his team as an integral part of the company, but in reality it is an isolated pocket of excellence. Although the company has no clear vision, he developed one for his group. He views team members as valuable participants and reminds them to keep their skill sets current so that they will always have a niche inside or outside the company. He rewards them by including them as coauthors of presentations and professional papers and providing them with visibility within the company. He thinks that the team provides its members with a sense of community and safety.

Mavericks like Carlos consistently take responsibility for:

- Providing their people with a clear vision, direction, and boundaries
- Running interference for them within the organization
- Acting as coaches for them
- Providing them with the information they need to make informed decisions
- Creating a safe and supportive environment for them

Rob, a technical-service manager at a large computer company, tells us that a big part of his job is keeping his people together. Regardless of what other managers do, he has decided he wants his people to feel that they are not alone. He has given them a vision and the authority to use it as a decision-making tool. He tries to provide them with information and the resources they need.

Rob, Carlos, and others like them are creating their own oases within their organizations. Their results give them the leeway to try innovative practices. The following questions can help you begin to judge how your organization is doing in adopting a Free Agent mind set. You can use these questions as a guide to identifying your company's strengths as well as those areas that might need special attention.

- Do employees use the company mission statement as a basis for making daily decisions?
- Does the company mission inspire and motivate?
- Has the company built up myths that reinforce the vision?
- Do employees feel confident enough to make their own decisions?
- Are managers allowing their employees to solve problems during crises?

It is helpful when senior management and the infrastructure support managers' goals of creating and maintaining Free Agent communities. Kim-Lei feels her company could be much more successful if it took a systemic approach to creating a Free Agent community. To do that, however, the leaders would need to scrutinize and redefine their systems to make sure they met the needs of both Free Agents and the company. The next stage in our process for becoming a Free Agent community, Redefining, outlines such a redesign of the organization's infrastructure to support and build a Free Agent community.

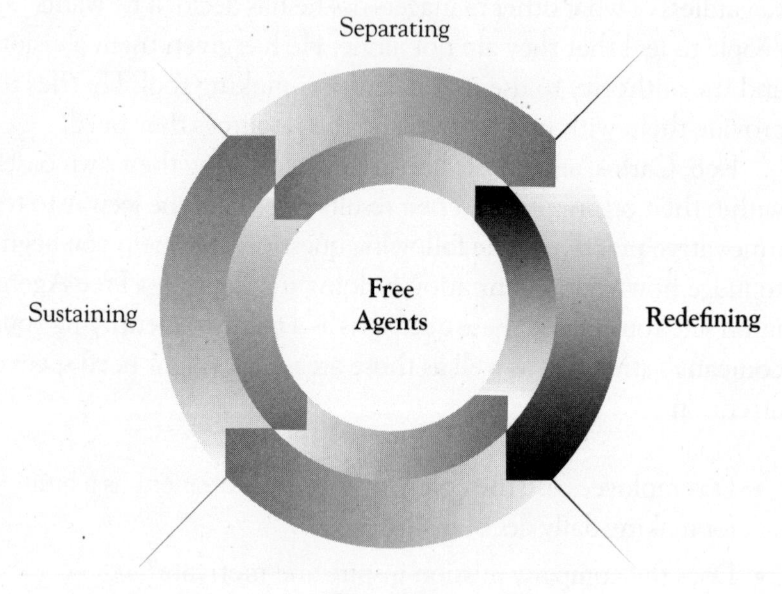
Separating
Sustaining
Free
Agents
Redefining
Positioning

## *Chapter Eight*

# Redefining the Corporate Infrastructure

> The rules of the marketplace may be cruel, but they have taught us three valuable lessons. If we rest on our laurels, we will wither. If we stop being bold, we will rot. If we don't take leaps of faith, we cannot lead.
>
> —*J. B. Martin, "UCSF Change and the High Road to Excellence"*

As the staff at Ellen's software company grew, she worried about developing an infrastructure that would meet employees' needs and those of the company. Her employees discussed the kind of atmosphere that would foster their enthusiasm, productivity, and commitment to the company's mission. What would the characteristics be of a workplace that supported innovation, creativity, and high levels of performance? Ellen realized that all the systems that made up the infrastructure of the company had to be designed to provide a strong foundation for such a community. *Redefining* for businesses is precisely this process of analyzing and refining or re-creating the company's infrastructure as the basis for a Free Agent community. In this stage companies design and build new systems that enable employees to make their best contribution to the company.

In the previous chapter we discussed the importance of creating a corporate vision that permeates every fiber of the organization. This vision becomes the crucial underpinning for each part of the company's infrastructure. When a company has a clear vision, the systems provide the structure for implementing that vision on a daily basis. Without a clearly defined vision, it becomes extremely difficult, if not impossible, to design systems that are cohesive, consistent, and interdependent (Collins and Porras, 1994, pp. 201–202). When a company endeavors to create a Free Agent community, it is essential that the communication, performance-management, compensation, and recognition systems be aligned.

## Communication Systems

> Information zips along an internal superhighway: . . . technology moves it quickly across the corporation instead of up and down, speeding up and improving decision making [Jacob, 1995, p. 91].

Once managers replace old convictions about safeguarding information with an understanding of the value of widespread dissemination, they are ready to Redefine their current communication systems. As we mentioned in Chapter Seven, they need to create systems that ensure broad and speedy distribution of a wide range of information throughout the organization. For example, one company sends daily activity statistics to all employees to maintain a focus on its customer-commitment objectives. Another reports information about cash flow on a weekly basis, which encourages all employees to pay attention to financial results. A third company shares ideas about innovative work practices across business units through their best-practice database developed in-house (Ashkenas, Ulrich, Jick, and Kerr, 1995, p. 75). One person's idea can immediately spark another's creativity and innovation. Because individuals are encouraged to take risks, this sharing of information and intelligence often fuels the development of new and better products and systems.

Three principles provide the rationale for rethinking and redesigning communication systems: Free Agents need information to do their jobs effectively; disseminating information encourages autonomy by permitting and enabling individuals to make their own decisions; Free Agents want and expect this type of independence in their workplaces.

As they redesign their communication systems, managers need to decide what information to share, how to deliver it, and how to help employees use it.

### *What Information to Share*

Because the economic future of Free Agents depends on the success of their organizations, they feel that they need to have the "big picture." Their companies' financial conditions and business decisions have a direct effect on their careers. Because Ellen wants her employees to keep the company's financial picture in mind all the time, she regularly highlights and distributes information on key financial levers, along with the appropriate operation and budget numbers. Her managers never think about who should or should not receive this information. Everyone in the company receives the reports. It is no longer useful for employees to learn about the company's finances once a year through the annual report. Free Agents need this information on a regular basis.

And by sharing potentially sensitive information—such as giving advance notice that the company will be shutting down certain operations—companies can solicit valuable input from Free Agents. As an example, a company recently decided to outsource an entire area of the business. Managers shared this information with their workers four months in advance. Employees were offered either a severance package if they stayed to the end or a temporary project assignment until they found another opportunity inside or outside the company. To the managers' surprise, employees began making good suggestions for the transition, and most of them stayed until the end. Those who decided to leave early shared their exit plans so that the company was able to find ways to manage without them (Waterman, Waterman, and Collard, 1994, pp. 92–93).

Managers should keep in mind the necessity of sharing a balance of good and bad news so that employees will have a realistic understanding of how the company is doing. Good news motivates and inspires; bad news reduces unpleasant surprises but also blocks out positive messages. When "pessimists harp on problems, . . . employees never hear the good news" (Ashkenas, Ulrich, Jick, and Kerr, 1995, p. 77).

### *How to Deliver Information*

Companies that are redesigning their infrastructure want their whole workforce to receive information quickly so that they can use it immediately in their work and decision making. Matching the message to the many modes of delivery that are available results in the most effective communication. For example, fliers, memos, and on-line bulletins work well for sharing factual information. Small group meetings are more effective for giving people the information they need to change their behavior (Ashkenas, Ulrich, Jick, and Kerr, 1995, p. 75).

New technology makes the widespread, speedy delivery of information much easier than it used to be. E-mail or variations of on-line services and networks are indispensable because everyone receives the same information at once and across geographical boundaries. These methods of delivery support coordination and collaboration and provide the means for updating information quickly (Levine, 1996, pp. 2A, 4A). Attention to the amount of data being sent guards against creating information overload.

### *How to Help Employees Use Information*

Having access to information is only the first step. Comprehending and using the information are equally important. Companies want to ensure that everyone is able to interpret the information and translate it into action. They help employees understand what the financial information means to competitors, to the business, to their specific position, and to them personally. Some companies run formal training classes on how to understand the key data essential for managing the business and how to interpret financial information because they want their employees to grasp the financial impact of all the decisions they make. Other teaching resources include business education videos, suggested readings, and software and self-paced programs. Understanding the business also enables Free Agents to become excited about helping the company grow and succeed. It creates the foundation for feeling connected and enfranchised (Case, 1995, pp. 75–84).

## Performance-Management Systems

Traditionally, the purpose of performance-management systems was to provide a rationale and legitimacy for a system that rewarded long-term employment and was characterized by promotion ladders and individual job titles (Ancona and others, 1996, p. 12). Once a year managers filled out evaluation forms and then met with their employees to explain them. As the business landscape changes, this system no longer works. The new demands for heightened performance, flexibility, and teamwork are causing companies to redefine their performance systems to ensure that objectives are clearly aligned with the corporate vision, are focused on effectiveness, and measure individual and team accomplishments.

Free Agents want to be involved in managing their performance, and they like to give feedback to and receive it from other employees on their team. They want to participate in setting their objectives and identifying the criteria against which whey will be evaluated. They believe objectives should be clear and measurable and should focus on results. They want these individual and team objectives directly tied to corporate goals, and they want them to encourage joint problem solving. These measurements can then be used to guide and reinforce performance, indicate problems, and identify skills needed for career development.

Such a system becomes a powerful management tool for controlling work rather than the individual. It recognizes that Free

Agents require less monitoring and more support and coaching than former employees did.

Assessments that use many evaluators supply rich feedback through multiple perspectives about an employee's performance (O'Reilly, 1994b, p. 93). When Mike took his current position as CEO of a medical-device manufacturing company, he implemented a 360–degree feedback system that allows selected team members, peers, managers, and customers to assess individual performance. It also provides a picture of how individuals fit into a team by measuring the "softer," more personal skills in addition to technical expertise. Because people find constructive feedback easier to receive from more than one person, this approach seems more objective and less threatening.

When and how often should individual and team performance be evaluated? Ellen's managers decided that timely assessment was critical. They link their appraisals to project cycles rather than to annual pay increases so that Free Agents can receive feedback that is helpful on subsequent projects. This appraisal includes feedback from each team member, not just one individual. As one manager explains, "It's kind of like the Monday morning after a game. We analyze what transpired and identify what we did well and what we can do better next time." In another company, informal appraisals are conducted after each project or when the task is completed, and formal appraisals are conducted annually.

Regardless of the timing of the appraisals, they should focus on progress and problems: what has been achieved since the last evaluation and what has impeded progress or might be an early warning of a problem. This kind of appraisal avoids costly crises by detecting and handling problems early. And it creates an environment of mutual trust and continuous learning. Appraisals become a tool for internal Free Agents to use in tracking their own development. Legal issues make it difficult for companies to include external Free Agents in evaluations unless they initiate the process themselves (see Chapter Ten).

## Compensation Systems

Compensation encompasses many different factors. Combining these factors in the right way can motivate short-and long-term performance. These factors include salary, benefits, raises, bonuses, commissions, stock options, and restricted stock grants. The goal of any compensation system is to pay fairly for performance that favorably affects the company's bottom line.

Compensation can be an important factor in attracting a Free Agent workforce. Because a Free Agent has a choice of where to work and knows his or her value in the marketplace, companies need to design compensation systems that give them the ability to obtain and retain the skills they demand.

In the past, compensation systems were not always directly tied to performance and results. Often individuals were compensated for seniority and average work rather than for superior outcomes. Salary increases tended to cluster in a narrow range with little distinction between good and poor performance. This system does not work in a competitive, results-oriented marketplace. Free Agents want and expect compensation systems that are linked to individual and team skills and performance, and to how well they outperform competitors.

Many companies are struggling with the challenges of redesigning their compensation systems to reward behavior that is aligned with the values of the new community. Keep in mind that compensation is a formidable issue; there are no simple solutions to many of the problems it poses. Human resource professionals know that a successful compensation system aligns individual and corporate interests—never an easy task. Compensation must be examined frequently and changed as necessary in order to provide the appropriate incentives. At the same time, the system must be flexible. If the company changes or does not grow at the expected rate, the compensation package has to reflect these changes.

Despite the difficulty of devising successful and fair compensation systems, meeting the following criteria can be a good way to start.

1. *Include both base and variable compensation components*. Many companies are searching for a way to get away from the traditional, standard-percentage, annual pay increase. The solution for some is a variable-pay plan, which combines base pay with an "at risk" portion. These plans typically tie bonuses to one or more of three measures: the performance of the entire company, the results of a business unit, or the results of the individual (Tully, 1993, p. 88). In these plans the base pay could be lower than the industry average, but individuals could end up earning more through their bonus pay.

Often, a companywide bonus system is too distant to motivate performance. Free Agents want to be judged on outcomes they can affect directly. Because Free Agents work in a project-based world, they need to be rewarded for completing projects on time and within budget. Therefore, they often prefer their variable pay to reflect the results of the team or business unit rather than the entire company. In one company, 70 percent of each manager's bonus depends on the unit's results, and the other 30 percent is based on individual and team success (Tully, 1993, p. 95).

When Mike's senior management team was redesigning the compensation system, they developed a variable-pay plan that would encourage their managers to produce outstanding earnings. To receive the bonus, managers needed to exceed the previous year's earnings of their business units by a minimum of 10 percent. Less than the desired minimum increase resulted in base salary only. Any increase over the 10 percent resulted in bonuses. The company extended eligibility to more people in the organization than previously and agreed to review the results at the beginning of the next fiscal year.

Companies are trying various ways to divide the base and variable percentages. Two points of agreement are that the base compensation needs to be tied to the complexity of the function and the required skills and that the variable portion needs to be based on both individual and team contributions.

2. *Tie rewards to the company's bottom line and goals*. Free Agents are motivated when rewards are linked to the accomplishment of key objectives, completion of important projects, and improvements in the company's competitive position. When planning such rewards, managers need to be sure that the results they are rewarding are ones employees can directly affect.

3. *Reward team as well as individual outcomes*. Free Agents benefit from being part of a team and understanding their role as team members. They expect that they will be compensated in part for team outcomes. They believe in shared successes and shared failures. Although sharing rewards sound attractive, it is difficult to make operational. Issues of fairness and increased competition among team members present obstacles. Later in this chapter we raise important questions to consider when setting up team rewards.

4. *Pay for individual contributions*. Free Agents expect to be compensated for their skills and their value to the organization at levels that are comparable to those in the marketplace. More and more companies are discovering the importance of targeting and specifically rewarding the skills and outcomes they need to survive and prosper. One strategy is to offer bonuses and incentives to individuals throughout the organization who make vital contributions and develop critical new skills, regardless of level. For example, some companies are providing their technical people, considered to be the value creators critical to the company's success, with compensation and bonus programs that enable them to earn a significantly greater amount than their managers. Paying for contributions de-emphasizes vertical advancement and encourages lateral movement and skill development (Ancona and others, 1996, p. 12).

5. *Design incentives to encourage both short-and long-term outcomes*. Variable-pay plans offer alternatives for obtaining results and rewarding performance. Bonuses usually reward the achievement

of short-term goals, such as cutting inventory or meeting project deadlines and budgets. Stock options act as long-term motivators. In the past they were reserved primarily for senior managers who had long-term strategic responsibilities. Now companies are experimenting with offering both bonuses and stock options as incentives for more of their employees (Tully, 1993, p. 84).

Viewing compensation in this way represents a new approach and raises some substantive questions that need attention.

- Are you rewarding the skills that are critical to the company?
- Are you motivating and rewarding individuals for lateral moves?
- How do you resolve the conflict between the company values of collaboration and cooperation and inter-team competition?
- What criteria do you use for rewarding team members? Are rewards distributed equally among team members, distributed in proportion to individual contributions, or distributed in some other fair way?
- How do you measure contributions? Time spent on the project? Effort exerted? Quality of ideas contributed? Technical value of the skills? (Ancona and others, 1996, p. 12)

The process for developing and implementing compensation systems is also changing. For these systems to work, companies must get buy-in from their workforce. Today compensation plans need to be presented to employees and their feedback needs to be solicited so that they have a sense of ownership. The entire workforce can be turned off if compensation is not handled the right way (Fierman, 1994b, p. 61).

In addition, employees need to know what is included in their compensation. Ellen's employees are paid well because she wants everyone to share in the company's success. Stock-option grants, company-paid retirement funding, bonuses, and profit-sharing programs are all included in the compensation package. The company lists the value of each component of the total compensation, including benefits received, on the stub of each paycheck so that employees know what the company is doing for them.

## Reward and Recognition Systems

> People are surprisingly harsh on themselves when it comes to saying what salary increase they should get. Many say they are satisfied and that they want something nonsalary related such as a faster computer, a larger office, an additional staff member. In fact, I hear this many more times than I hear "I want extra stock options and more money."

Reward and recognition systems can be powerful motivators in directing and reinforcing performance. In the past managers have not always taken full advantage of these tools, even though for many years behavioral and industrial psychologists have been saying that individuals are driven more by recognition than by money. Free Agents want and need to be recognized for their accomplishments, contributions, and expertise. The rewards can be small or large, tangible or intangible, public or private, but the recognition needs to be explicit.

Ellen knows that in her company some individuals enjoy public recognition for a job well done. They are saluted in the company on-line newsletter. But for others such recognition would be too overwhelming, so their team leaders write them a personal thank you note or give them a gift certificate for a free dinner.

In general, a Free Agent reward and recognition system should:

- Recognize individual and team contributions, leadership, accomplishments, and expertise
- Reward accomplishments that are aligned with company goals and strategies
- Reinforce behaviors and performance in a timely manner
- Include external Free Agents
- Be perceived as fairly and consistently applied

Recognition takes many forms. Some of the best rewards are intangible, while others are tangible but relatively inexpensive. Here are a few suggestions:

- Recognize the expertise that Free Agents bring to their work by asking them for advice and counsel.
- Involve Free Agents in decision making, particularly on team projects.
- Spotlight accomplishments by posting letters of commendation on a visible bulletin board, assigning the employee being rewarded to desirable projects, designating an employee-of-the-month parking space, featuring success stories in a newsletter or on e-mail.
- Give small gifts—flowers or dinners—repeatedly and consistently.
- Include external Free Agents in meetings, events, decisions as much as possible and treat them like valuable members of the group.
- Use company recognition programs often.

Recognition is a critical part of managers' jobs. Managers should be encouraged to provide all types of reinforcement on an ongoing basis and should be given the tools they need—resources and money—to provide the rewards their people deserve. A part of their performance appraisal should be based on how effective they are at providing recognition.

The following questions are important to ask repeatedly as you build your Free Agent community:

- Are your internal hotlines or other communication vehicles used regularly to share news quickly?
- Do you make sure that important information stands out and gets attention?

- Do individuals and teams tie their decisions to the company's financial targets?
- Are managers evaluated on their ability to deliver timely and objective performance evaluations?
- Do people use feedback as a basis for changing behavior?
- Has collaboration between individuals and teams increased over the last year?
- Do your value creators feel fully rewarded and appreciated?

Companies are recognizing the need for building an infrastructure that links Free Agents to common shared values and vision. The systems support the vision on an operational level and create continuity and affinity. They create the network that unites Free Agents and results in a community of purpose. Such a community has a simple basis: clear expectations, mutual respect, fairness, and appreciation. When these values are supported by every system, individuals will be motivated to do their best. In Ellen's company, every time management makes a decision about any system, they always ask themselves: What message are we giving? What does this say about how we feel about our employees? How does this affect our other systems? Infrastructure created in this way is key to the complex and difficult task of Positioning your company in the marketplace as a haven for Free Agents—the topic of the next chapter.

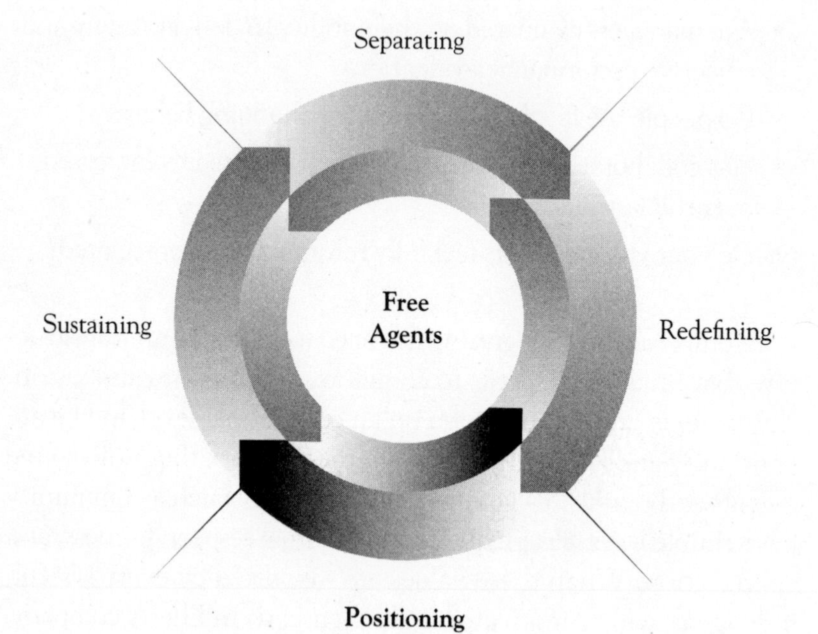
Separating
Sustaining
Free
Agents
Redefining
Positioning

## *Chapter Nine*

# Corporate Positioning

> We invest a lot of time and money in our hiring process. We want to ensure that we get the best people for our company and that they choose to come to work here. We look for the right skills, attitudes, and a belief in our vision and core values. We get buy-in for candidates across all departments and at all levels. Everyone talks about how grueling it is; but when we do hire, we all know that it's going to be a good fit.

In the previous chapter we looked at how some companies are Redefining their systems that serve as the foundation for their Free Agent communities. In addition, these companies are aware that their ability to secure critical skills depends on how they are viewed in the marketplace. For this reason, they are exploring additional systems that will enable them to build and maintain environments where Free Agents want to work.

Determining how to compete for talent is the next stage in our process, *Positioning*. The focus of the Positioning stage is primarily external. How will the company be perceived from outside? Will it be the company of choice for Free Agents? In this stage, a company makes sure that it has the capability to recruit, hire, and develop the individuals who are right for the organization.

Ellen explained that her company is dependent on its human assets. From the beginning her staff realized how competitive the marketplace was for the individuals they wanted; they could not afford any negative press in the Free Agent network. They also knew that a bad hiring decision is terribly costly because of the time invested in the hiring process and in training the new employee. For these reasons, developing a process for hiring the right people was mandatory, and they designed and implemented a system for doing so.

Everyone on project teams in Ellen's company is directly involved in hiring new members. Together they identify the skills and personal characteristics that are critical to a specific project. All team members receive training in interviewing so that everyone is competent to evaluate the candidates' suitability. When a hiring decision does not work out well, the team takes responsibility for analyzing what went wrong and determining how to avoid that mistake next time.

Ellen believes that this approach is one of the keys to the company's success and growth. She finds that rapid changes in the marketplace force the company to reassess skill needs often and to make the necessary adjustments in its hiring practices.

The Positioning stage is also the time to look at other practices that influence a company's reputation in the marketplace: matching skills to corporate needs, providing professional-development opportunities for Free Agents, and making it easy for people to leave. The remainder of this chapter explores these practices.

## Matching Skills to Corporate Needs

More than ever before managers are looking carefully at the skills that are critical for their businesses and are clearly defining the skills they have to obtain from the outside and the ones they can develop in-house. This enables them to provide their current and prospective employees with clear expectations about the work that needs to be done and the opportunities for learning and development. As companies are increasingly defining their work around projects rather than functions, the emphasis is on quickly assembling skill-based teams (Dent, 1995, p. 26).

On these teams, companies need people who:

- Have the appropriate functional skills as well as strong leadership, interpersonal, and communication skills
- Have cross-functional capabilities
- Seek out opportunities to learn new skills
- Understand overall business and customer needs
- Deal well with ambiguity
- Have the ability to influence people over whom they do not have direct authority
- Fit into the team culture

When asked what she looks for in candidates, a vice president for executive recruitment explains that her company needs individuals who not only have specialized skills but, above all else, are flexible and resilient. They need to work well on different project teams simultaneously and be able to rearrange priorities and let go of projects in response to market needs.

Individuals with this broadened skill base are able to move from project to project and are comfortable switching back and forth between regular duties and special projects (Waterman, Waterman, and Collard, 1994, p. 88). Work rotation provides flexibility for the organization because the same group of people can be reconfigured to accomplish a number of different tasks. Such flexibility enables organizations to meet changing customer needs. It is also attractive to Free Agents, who like the opportunity to change roles and use different skills—from being individual contributors to being team leaders to being managers. This practice benefits them by providing them with the opportunity to add to their Portfolio of Assets.

Ellen explains that in her company some people have been in and out of management for the past seven years. Although all like being managers, being individual contributors gives them the chance to update their technical skills. They can work on many interesting projects and use their specialized knowledge. Rotating jobs in this way also enables other individuals to expand their capabilities by assuming management functions. This is a big selling point for the company when these individuals talk to other members of their networks.

This new focus on skills benefits everyone. By understanding the skills the business needs current employees can be proactive about charting their path in the company. Developing internal talent whenever possible rather than constantly bringing new players on board is good for the company and good for morale.

A project and skill focus encourages companies to allocate resources for identifying and keeping track of the skills available within their organizations. Software programs can track internal skill profiles and develop skill-based job descriptions. These programs require employees to identify and list their skills and put them into the company data bank.

When information is centralized in this way, managers can accurately and quickly match project needs with the skill sets of individuals within the company. Employees can determine the skills they need for future opportunities. And because all these practices require individuals to identify and update their Portfolio of Assets, they encourage everyone in the organization to think of themselves in terms of skills rather than job titles. This is a key step in becoming Free Agents.

## Updating Recruiting and Hiring Systems

Another reason for matching skills companies need with individual talents is to improve hiring decisions. When companies are able to rationalize their hiring practices in this way, individuals can make the best use of their talents, and they feel valued because the company is investing in their development. Companies can bring in people with the right skills and thereby reduce costly mistakes and disruption to the existing community.

As people are seen increasingly as assets rather than as interchangeable commodities, recruiters are gaining importance in the community-building process. The partnership among recruiters, human resource professionals, and hiring managers is strengthened as they all focus on developing the job descriptions and finding the people with the skills sets they need. Managers we interviewed consider their recruiters and their human resource people as their companies' marketing arm as well as their sales force in the hiring process.

Because these professionals are selling their companies in competitive marketplaces, they are expected and trained to understand many different aspects of the company. They have to keep abreast of industry changes and trends and their impact on the company and its corporate strategy. As salespeople they have to knowledgeably present to candidates the required skills, the compensation structure, and the career-development opportunities. They must accurately describe the corporate values and culture. Along with hiring managers, they must be able to put together and negotiate competitive offers because candidates may have several others in hand. If the recruiter cannot help to close the deal, the company has lost time, energy, money, and the right person.

Ellen's company relies on two recruiters. They know every aspect of Ellen's industry and of her business from products to financial projections. They work closely with project teams to identify skills. They rely on everyone in the company for recommendations; anyone can receive financial rewards when people they refer are hired.

The hiring process itself is also changing. Because poor hiring decisions undermine and have a negative impact on community, some companies conduct time-consuming, multiple interviews with every candidate. Candidates meet with team managers and project leaders, team members, other potential colleagues, and, sometimes, the CEO. To facilitate good hiring decisions, Ellen requires her managers to attend three-day training sessions on interviewing techniques.

Companies use these interviews to further explore technical and functional skills as well as the candidate's ability to fit into the company. The goal is to explain company values, to describe the work itself, and to find out whether the individual's needs are aligned with the company's and whether the person belongs on the team and in the community. Managers attempting to build Free Agent communities understand that hiring decisions do not work out when individuals' ambitions do not fit with the available development opportunities, individuals' styles do not fit with the company's culture, and individuals' expectations are not met.

Describing a company's culture clearly and accurately to potential employees helps to avoid such errors. A CEO we interviewed described his company as hard-driving. Employees do not spend a lot of time talking about their work, they just do it. Managers warn job candidates not to expect a lot of warm fuzzies; in this organization, the absence of criticism is considered praise. The CEO recognizes that some people do not do well in this kind of environment and feels they should have enough information to decide whether it is the place for them.

A human resource director told us about a job candidate who was brilliant and talented. Everyone was bowled over. At the end of a day of intensive interviews, the company made him an immediate offer. He said he would think about it, but he was quite sure he would not accept. Upon further probing, he explained that he could not stand the open, unstructured environment represented by the cubicles with no doors. Sometime later, the director happened to attend a meeting at the company this individual eventually joined. She noticed that his office had an anteroom with a door on it and that he was sitting in his office with the door closed and his headphones on. The director knew this individual had made exactly the right decision. He would never have been happy in their participative and interactive culture, where the managers were expected to be out with their people at all times.

In sum, managers offered these suggestions for attracting new members of a Free Agent community:

- Clearly articulate the company's philosophy and practices early in the process
- Describe the company and the business in detail
- Explain what managers expect of all employees and what their employees can expect from them
- Explain concisely and accurately the position, the work, the opportunities for professional development, and the criteria for success

A hiring process based on these suggestions assists managers to match individuals with company expectations. And, at the same time, individuals have a good basis for deciding whether the company will meet their expectations.

## Providing Development Opportunities

> Each person who comes to work here gets about three to four weeks of training during the first four months. We try to impart the message that we really care about employees' ability to grow professionally.

Providing development opportunities is important in attracting and retaining Free Agents, especially for companies that cannot offer their employees rapid advancement. Harvard professor Shoshanna Zuboff, author of *In the Age of the Smart Machine*, says, "The 21st century company has to promote and nurture the capacity to improve and to innovate. . . . [This] means [that] learning becomes the axial principle of organizations. It replaces control as the fundamental job of management" (quoted in Stewart, 1992, p. 94). In these companies learning and development are ongoing.

One CEO told us that training is so important to him and to his company that he attends every kickoff session for the management-training programs. All employees spend at least 5 percent of their time annually on education or training. He estimates that his company has a return of twenty dollars for each dollar it spends on employee development.

By encouraging and facilitating continuous learning for all employees, companies accrue a number of benefits: they remain dynamic and competitive, enhance their ability to change, motivate Free Agents by making them feel valued, improve their ability to attract new employees, increase employees' commitment to the team or the project.

To reap these rewards, companies need to invest in employee development. Their managers must be responsible for formulating development plans with their employees to map out specific skills they need to acquire. Providing the opportunity to attend formal training classes, rotate jobs, or participate in special assignments or cross-functional teams helps Free Agents develop a wide range of skills. These might include skills that help them work better on teams such as negotiating, listening, multi-tasking, and communicating cross-culturally (Ancona and others, 1996, pp. 12–17).

Some companies promote the idea of career resiliency, which is based on the belief that employees and employers share the responsibility for maintaining and even enhancing the individuals' employability both inside and outside the company. If companies expect employees to become Free Agents by continuously redefining and upgrading their skills, they have to provide them with the time, funding, coaching, and technology they need to expand their Portfolios of Assets. Some companies have internal career-management centers where Free Agents can receive assessments, counseling, and training. Counselors in these centers assist Free Agents in developing strategies for their careers; they provide reference materials and internal and external job listings (Waterman, Waterman, and Collard, 1994, p. 93). Companies without internal resource centers sometimes provide their employees with the opportunity to obtain these services externally. Or they implement an "electronic campus" that uses a computer network to gather career information and make it readily available. Such programs need to be fully supported by management at all levels (Waterman, Waterman, and Collard, 1994, p. 94).

## Making It Easy for People to Leave

People leave positions and companies for a variety of reasons. Perhaps they have the right skills but do not fit into the organization's culture. Or maybe they realize that they do not have the right talents. Sometimes they find another opportunity, even within the company, that enables them to enhance their skills more quickly.

In the past, a stigma was often attached to individuals who left. They were seen as disloyal; their colleagues and their company felt rejected. Even now managers who have traditional ideas think they have failed if their people leave. Free Agent organizations, however, recast their expectations in this regard and make it easy for people to move on. Many companies now expect that Free Agents will leave when they no longer provide value to the company or the company no longer provides them with learning opportunities. At the same time, they want these employees to be able to return if conditions change and mutual needs can once again be met. Mike's company has a no-fault-exit policy. When people leave, the company goes out of its way to make sure that the parting is amicable.

We are aware of companies where managers conduct in-depth exit interviews. They are interested in knowing why individuals are leaving and in obtaining useful feedback about their organizations. Even when people leave, the company extends membership in its community by maintaining contact and, in some instances, inviting these people back to educational events. Mike clearly explains:

> In the past when people left managers often took it very personally—they felt rejected. In our organization we see leaving as a normal part of the process of building and sustaining a dynamic community. The important thing is to find out why people are leaving. Is it us? Is it them? Or is it a better opportunity? We want our managers to help people to leave if it is best for the individual and the company. We find time and again that if we give people

> permission to move on to other opportunities, they return to us with even more valuable skills and experiences. When people feel good about looking out for themselves, they actually are also looking out for our company.

Such a policy has two advantages. The company gains a reputation as a good place to work and thus can continue to attract talented individuals. And past employees feel free to return, often bringing with them an enhanced skill base and greater motivation and enthusiasm.

## The Benefits

Companies that identify the skills they need, refine their recruiting and hiring practices, develop their people, and make it easy for individuals to leave when necessary become known for valuing their people and investing in them. Free Agents appreciate managers who go out of their way to increase their employability. When companies are in fierce competition for the same talents and skills, this strategy often provides the edge.

You can use the following questions as a guide to identify your company's strengths in attracting Free Agents, as well as those areas that might need special attention:

- Is there a "buzz" about your company that attracts a large applicant pool?
- Are significant numbers of people taking advantage of internal training and tuition-reimbursement programs?
- Do you have low turnover among new hires?
- Are all employees willing to serve on interview teams when asked?
- Are managers evaluated on their ability to develop their people?
- Do senior managers voluntarily and enthusiastically kick off training programs? Do they informally attend other programs?

- Do individuals seek opportunities to rotate jobs and to participate in special projects or on cross-functional teams?
- Have referrals by employees for job openings increased over the last year?
- Do you use the information you gather from exit interviews to modify your practices?
- Does your company have an active and supportive alumni group of former employees?

As organizations go through the Separating, Redefining, and Positioning stages of our process, they create a climate that is attractive to Free Agents: skills and talents are appreciated and supported; management beliefs and practices stimulate rather than hinder productivity and creativity; and Free Agents can find others with common values and a common purpose.

Creating a Free Agent community is only the beginning, however. Sustaining it over time takes care and nurturing. Part Three explains how individuals and corporations experience the last, and in some ways the most demanding, stage of our process, Sustaining.

Part Three

# *Sustaining Free Agents and a Free Agent Community*

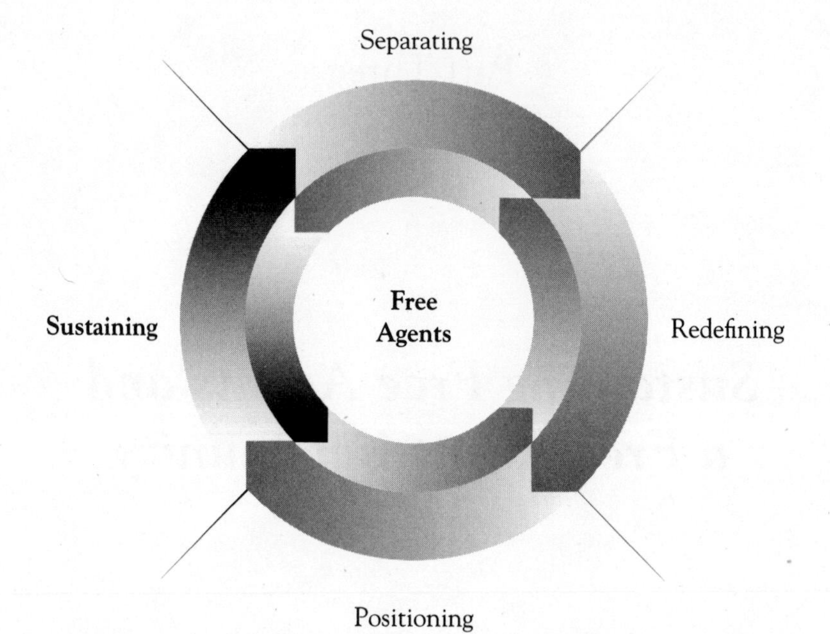
Separating
Free
Agents
Sustaining
Redefining
Positioning

*Chapter Ten*

# Living the Free Agent Life

> Dynamic and energetic is the way I would characterize the Free Agents I know. These people understand what they want and how to achieve it. They have a solid plan for achieving their goals. What impresses me is that they know where they are headed and how they will get there. They are secure in their ability to execute their plan over time.

We have devoted Part Three to the *Sustaining* stage of the process because it is so important for both individuals and corporations. For those who have achieved career independence and are establishing new relationships with the marketplace, the Sustaining stage is indispensable. It provides the tools and strategies for continuing as a Free Agent. Sustaining is a time for making a commitment to reviewing and reevaluating. To remain Free Agents individuals must diligently repeat the Redefining and Positioning stages, which involves researching new and emerging markets and reevaluating skills in order to ensure future employability. Free Agents have to be prepared to clearly explain their Portfolio of Assets and value to a new customer at all times.

To sustain a Free Agent community, a company must also commit to reviewing and reevaluating. Senior management needs to reassess the organization's mission and systems regularly. Is the company attracting and retaining the skilled people it needs? Is it achieving required results? Are the existing systems creating the best environment for Free Agents? Are there opportunities for continued learning? What changes or adjustments need to be made? Like individuals, companies have to commit to repeating Redefining and Positioning and then to making necessary changes to maintain community.

For most people and companies, Sustaining is consistently difficult. The other phases of the Free Agent process have an end. But Sustaining does not; it is a continuous process. The lack of an ending makes people uncomfortable in this stage; they want to reach a final destination, a resting point. They expect to go through this process just once and have their careers fixed forever so that they do not have to experience any more upheaval. But Sustaining does not work that way. Individuals and corporations must commit to a lifelong Free Agent process.

This chapter and the next describe the Sustaining stage, explore the feelings and challenges it presents, and outline strategies for success. We highlight the synergy that can result when individuals and corporations are working together toward maintaining a community. As in the first part of the book, we once again begin with the individual. When individuals are committed to remaining Free Agents, their companies are motivated to remain Free Agent communities.

## Why Commit to Being a Free Agent for Life?

Sustaining is the time to firmly commit to being a Free Agent for the rest of your working life. This commitment involves regularly leveraging your marketable skills, expanding your Portfolio of Assets, identifying new and emerging markets and seizing opportunities, and maintaining and building networks and support systems.

Those who resolve to remain Free Agents know that the search for lifetime employment, a steady paycheck, and other job guarantees is over. Security for Free Agents comes from knowing that they can market themselves, sell their skills, and be in control of their careers.

What keeps people motivated to maintain their Free Agent status? Eric, a financial analyst, is convinced that he has to remain a Free Agent because there is no assurance of a clear, steady career path. He cannot remember making a conscious choice to remain a Free Agent. As he went through the process, he simply found that he began viewing work in a completely different way. Now he feels confident about being responsible for his own career.

Lily, a backroom manager in a brokerage firm, used to worry about losing her job all the time. Today, she feels a new sense of freedom. Instead of thinking that the company has to take care of her, she is convinced that with her wide network and her ability to describe her assets, she can always find a place for herself. Becoming a Free Agent has empowered her. "People who have not seen me for a while, cannot believe I am the same person I was five years ago."

Others are motivated by the satisfaction of having interesting work. Felicia, an insurance company administrator, explains that 70 percent of her job is routine, but the other 30 percent, which she created herself, is always exciting. Felicia is confident that she can continue to make her work rewarding because she keeps up with what is happening in the company and she is adept at selling herself.

Free Agents' passion for learning plays an important role in their decision to remain Free Agents. They usually have a deep need to expand their skill sets and Portfolios of Assets. Free Agents take advantage of every opportunity to pick up a new skill and to learn from one another. As one multimedia developer put it, "I learn new skills all the time because I always want to be ahead and on the cutting edge."

## The Free Agent Life

At first the lack of security was very frightening. I would work so hard and become so invested in my project that I did not have any time to look for additional work. When the project ended, I would find myself once again looking for my next assignment.

The Free Agent life is volatile and unpredictable. Individuals who maintain their Free Agent status tend to be independent thinkers. Their confidence in their ability to shape their future and to succeed gives them the strength to deal with the uncertainty of the Free Agent life.

In addition to being volatile, the Free Agent way of life involves hard work. In order to maintain their worth in the market, Free Agents need routinely to

- Research new applications for their skills
- Identify and study new markets
- Expand their Portfolios of Assets to meet new and emerging needs
- Search for challenging and interesting work
- Take initiative and risks
- Remain flexible
- Maintain and build networks
- Build community

These tasks require a great deal of energy and a positive attitude.

Bob, a vice president whom we met in Chapter Two, says that regardless of his current position, he is always looking around inside and outside the company, doing research, and asking himself: What are the new markets? Where is the industry going? Where is this company going? What skills will I need next year? How can I make myself even more valuable to my organization?

## Feelings

Individuals who choose to remain Free Agents have to expect some unsettling feelings. Although it is challenging and exciting to be in charge of your career, you may feel frightened, anxious, and insecure.

Whether you are working on your own or in a company, completing a project with the next opportunity nowhere in sight can make you fearful and worried. You are faced with all that work to do over again: the reassessment of your Portfolio of Assets, the informational interviewing, the market research—to say nothing of finding yourself the right customer. You have no idea how long it will take or what the outcome will be. The first few episodes are the most frightening. As you experience success in finding your next client or your next company assignment, you will find the fears easier to deal with.

You may also feel insecure. No one is watching out for you; you are on your own. The slow periods in your business or the times when you need to move within or outside the company are especially nerve-wracking and make you wish you were back in a "secure" job. This is the time to reach out for support and encouragement. Sharing your feelings and hearing about how others cope can be helpful. Try not to let Alec's story, which follows, be yours.

Alec, a vice president at a large computer company, was out of work for about a year. During that period, he went through the process of becoming a Free Agent. He toyed with the idea of becoming an independent consultant. But the longer it took him to find work, the more frightened and insecure he became. Even though he had the financial resources to wait it out for at least another six months, when the first offer he called "a real job" came along, he grabbed it. A year of trying to be a Free Agent was over; he quickly sank back into old ways. He stopped networking and became so caught up in the job that he has paid no attention to expanding his skills. He is creating the same old box for himself. He has decided that he will stay in this position until retirement and sees no reason to continue to be a Free Agent. Perhaps Alec will be fortunate enough to realize his dream. More likely he will be looking for another "job" long before he retires.

## Challenges

It is important to talk about the difficulties and challenges so that people know what to expect. That way, when confronted, they will not feel surprised and dispirited. Talking about obstacles up front can help people figure out strategies ahead of time.

As you maintain Free Agent status, you can expect to face four main challenges: maintaining marketability, stretching yourself, maintaining balance, and dealing with finances.

### *Maintaining Marketability*

What you know and can do today will most likely not be enough in tomorrow's market. Technology and business requirements shift too quickly for anyone's Portfolio of Assets to have the same value in the future as it does today. The challenge is to know what you do well, identify what you need to learn, and find the resources to do it. You cannot always count on your company to provide training. As a Free Agent, your personal development is your responsibility. Only you can find the opportunities and decide how to take advantage of them.

Technology poses another set of problems. Everyone knows how important it is to keep up with the latest software and hardware developments. Still, taking the time to learn often goes to the bottom of the list. A determined engineer in a computer company says that his college-aged son was astonished to learn that his forty-six-year-old dad was taking evening classes at the local community college. "I told him that I expected to be going to school for the rest of my life. I do not have any other choice, do I?"

### *Stretching Yourself*

Another challenge is having to respond to the marketplace quickly. You must be ready to work in different markets and on different teams and projects. You need to act when a compelling opportunity presents itself. Going back and forth from nonmanagement to management responsibilities is an example of the personal flexibility that is required.

Although it may take extra effort, playing a variety of roles is a sure way to maintain a broad base of skills. Todd, who was trying to build a financial-management consulting business, had three projects with different sets of requirements. In one company he was restructuring the compensation package; in another he was providing a difficult internal audit; and for the third he was working as a part-time chief financial officer. Todd came close to turning down the chance to work on the compensation restructuring because he had never done it before. A colleague pointed out to him that he had the knowledge, he had just never applied it this way before. He then jumped at the chance to add this new skill to his Portfolio of Assets.

### *Maintaining Balance*

As a Free Agent you are your own boss and manager. Setting priorities, although often difficult to do, especially if your employer has always done it for you, is essential. There has to be a balance between what you need and want to do and the available hours in a day. For some it is a matter of avoiding burnout; for others it is a matter of juggling responsibilities. Lily and her husband struggle constantly with balance. They work long hours, have two small children, and want to remain Free Agents. Because they are always feeling overburdened, the temptation is not to undertake new projects. They resist this temptation by making a conscious decision to schedule at least one activity each week that sustains their Free Agent status. Lily might attend a special professional meeting or a community function; her husband might take a class or read business publications.

Among other benefits, setting priorities decreases the anxiety that strikes when you have an overwhelming number of things to do. Taking responsibility for structuring your day and making choices teaches you to keep your "must do" list short and to give yourself realistic time lines.

### *Dealing with Finances*

Free Agents realize that if they want to be in control of their careers, they must be in control of their finances. Financial insecurity rarely goes away. You cannot ever stop budgeting and contributing to your contingency fund. This financial cushion is invaluable. When you want to rethink your career direction, accept a lateral move within your company, or move to another company, the fund can relieve the fear and anxiety caused by decreased compensation. As we mentioned earlier, if you need help getting your finances in order, seek some professional advice.

Being a Free Agent means facing these challenges many times during your career. Those individuals who find it too difficult cease being Free Agents when the job crisis passes. Although they could have changed the way they think, they choose to return to a familiar place. They stop updating their skills, ignore their networks, and eventually settle into whatever job they can find. Like Alec, they hope that they can hang on until retirement. A manager in a large software company wants to do just the opposite. He admitted that in an industry where the majority of people are in their twenties and thirties, being fifty makes him old. "At my age, it is harder. But, I believe I am competitive, capable, and seasoned. I intend to keep moving forward."

## Strategies

> As Free Agents the only thing we really have control over is how we handle our situation strategically. Building networks and staying up to date are our keys to ongoing success.

The strategies for Sustaining the commitment to remaining a Free Agent are the same as those for becoming one. You just have to continue using them. If you can do nothing else, concentrate on these strategies to keep your momentum going: choose projects carefully, learn continuously, seek evaluations of your work, and build and maintain a network.

### *Choose Projects Carefully*

Because Free Agents are motivated by challenging and interesting work and are always trying to improve their position in the market, the projects and positions they choose are important. As a Free Agent you may have a variety of reasons for your choice. One position may increase your visibility within the division, company, or professional group. Another may offer the chance to be part of a cross-functional team so that you can learn how other parts of the organization operate. A third may enable you to learn a new skill.

Any project you choose should have clearly defined goals, roles, and expectations. As you select a project, think about whether it offers the opportunity to learn new skills and increase your knowledge, a new and unusual challenge, the opportunity to build and expand networks, the chance to use and learn about new technology, and the opportunity to provide value to the team and the company.

Internal Free Agents keep track of where the greatest resources are being assigned. Within this pool, they search out projects that meet their criteria and then take the initiative to get themselves assigned to those projects. External Free Agents have their antennae out to keep abreast of what is happening within industries and companies. They know which projects are on the cutting edge, and they go after a place on those teams. Darryl, a mid-level manager, recently pursued an opening that was posted in the company career center. Two of his peers with skills similar to his were also interested in the position, but neither actively went after the assignment. Darryl took the initiative because he realized immediately that the position offered a good chance to acquire additional skills and network more broadly within the organization.

### *Learn Continuously*

New technologies are making skills obsolete at a frightening pace. Businesses today are looking for people who are open to learning all the time. A manager in a large utility company sums up, "You are never going to lose the need for accelerated skill development. You absolutely can't read enough, you can't learn enough; performance is still the key. You've just got to be constantly increasing your knowledge and finding ways to let people know you have the knowledge to be successful. If you want to be well respected, if you want to be taken seriously and have credibility, you've got to have the broadest base of knowledge possible."

Free Agents find ways to keep their skills current. As we mentioned in the previous chapter, internal Free Agents get themselves assigned to cross-functional teams, rotate jobs, and seek out special assignments in order to acquire new skills. External Free Agents team up with specialists in related areas and are always ready to learn new skills as they work on projects.

Grace, a graphic designer, agreed to team up with two other external Free Agents to develop a multimedia presentation for a national sales conference. She was excited because the project would expose her to new technology. Not only was that expectation met, but she formed alliances with other Free Agents. She can now pull together her own team of specialists for future projects.

### *Seek Evaluations of Your Work*

If you are an external Free Agent, you probably will need to initiate performance reviews yourself; internal Free Agents should be sure that reviews are frequent enough and detailed enough to be helpful. In this process, focus on setting objectives and clarifying expectations. Schedule checkpoints throughout a project where you can review progress, obtain support and resources, and identify problems. For Free Agents, performance reviews are an integral part of managing themselves and their work.

### *Build and Maintain a Network*

Building and nurturing a network enables Free Agents to continue to market themselves, keep current, and share knowledge and information—critical strategies for remaining a Free Agent. They are aware that connections will lead to new markets and new opportunities. They cannot afford to allow their networks to stagnate.

Emily, a management consultant, acknowledges that she has not taken the time to keep up her network. On the one hand, she is concerned about spending time and money on networking when she is not convinced it is important. And she does not like going to professional meetings or scheduling breakfasts and lunches. On the other hand, she feels isolated, and she knows her knowledge of the industry is dated. If Emily is to continue as a Free Agent, she has to reconcile these conflicting feelings.

Eric is an example of a Free Agent who is particularly adept at networking. He uses technology to keep in touch with a large number of people: e-mail to congratulate an old colleague who has just landed her dream position; voice mail with no answer required to let a mentor know the latest development in Eric's work situation; a chat room to exchange ideas with international colleagues. When he is looking for new markets for his Portfolio he uses online resources to identify executives within his targeted companies. He then searches for any common affiliations with these individuals to make the initial contact easier. He never passes up the chance to become part of someone else's network.

The Free Agent life becomes easier to maintain as you build and keep in touch with your network. When you are tempted to revert back to familiar patterns, your network can provide the support you need to sustain your Free Agent status.

The following practices can help you remain a Free Agent and in the process guarantee a position for yourself in the marketplace:

- Keep abreast of your industry and your company
- Follow press coverage of your industry and your company

- Keep in touch with your company's competitors and suppliers
- Compare the product or service you provide externally or internally with similar products being offered by others
- Ascertain where most resources are being allocated
- Redefine yourself often
- Ask yourself whether you would hire yourself
- Assess how you add value to your organization and what your customers value you for the most
- Make sure that you have information or knowledge that is critical to your company's competitiveness
- Offer your company perspectives that are unavailable elsewhere
- Understand your company's strategy and how your skills fit in
- Determine which skills the "stars" in your organization possess and make them part of your Portfolio
- Ask for frequent evaluations in order to monitor your performance and identify future areas for development
- Maintain your network
- Be sure your boss is your champion
- Cultivate champions and mentors outside your department and your company
- Act as a mentor for others
- Be active in professional organizations

## Are You a Committed Free Agent?

Have you made the commitment to remain a Free Agent? Some people know the answer immediately; for others the realization that they are committed to being a Free Agent is gradual. One client said she knew she was a Free Agent when she found herself convincing a friend who had recently lost her job to go through the Free Agent process.

We reproduce here the list of questions we introduced in Chapter Two. There, we suggested that you use it to determine whether you had become a Free Agent. Here, we suggest that you use it to determine whether you are committed to remaining one.

*The Free Agent Checklist*

_____ I look for opportunities in change.

_____ I accept the insecurity of a job.

_____ I am more vested in challenging work than in job titles.

_____ I see myself as self-employed at all times.

_____ I can clearly describe my strengths and marketable skills.

_____ I am continuously adding to my Portfolio of Assets.

_____ I always look for gaps and needs in the marketplace.

_____ I continuously look for new opportunities to market myself.

_____ I carefully choose new projects.

_____ I am always improving my ability to be a productive team member.

_____ I form networks and alliances to expand my capabilities.

_____ I am committed to remaining a Free Agent for life.

The effort to sustain your commitment to become and remain a Free Agent is enhanced when businesses share the responsibility for providing "training to help employees stay current, continue to learn new skills and remain employable" (Ancona and others, 1996, p. 10). The next chapter explores these ideas further.

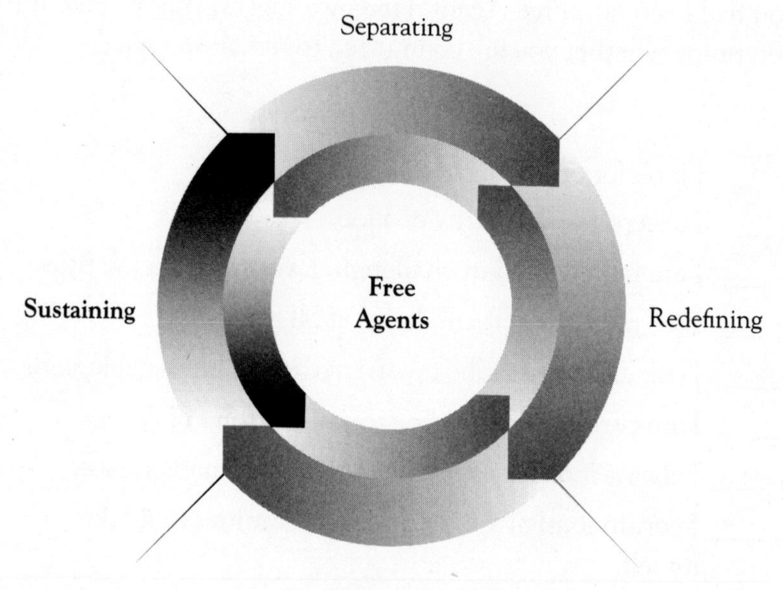
Separating
Sustaining
Free
Agents
Redefining
Positioning

*Chapter Eleven*

# Maintaining a Free Agent Community

Only a system tuned and calibrated to the needs of the moment produces wonderful music. In organizations, too, once the components are in place they need constant tuning.

—*R. Ashkenas, D. Ulrich, T. Jick, and S. Kerr,*
The Boundaryless Organization

Ellen is sitting in her office, reading the results of the company's annual employee-satisfaction surveys. Everything looks good: communication systems are fine; regard for the quality of the products is high; professional development plans are being implemented; and managers are providing timely and constructive feedback. Then Ellen notices a red flag. She has already heard the grumblings in the halls. Everyone is upset about the variable-compensation plan that was implemented two months ago. Ellen had felt pressured by the board to make this change quickly; she did not have the time to gain employee acceptance. Uncharacteristically, she and her executive team had worked behind closed doors to sort out the details, and then they announced the plan to the rest of the company. And now people throughout the company are unhappy. They believe that the process for arriving at the new plan was contrary to the way they operated in the past. Furthermore, the plan itself does not support the corporate vision. Employees are convinced that the success of their business is the result of cooperation and team effort. The process for devising the new plan has made them feel disenfranchised and less in control. As she reads the surveys, Ellen begins to understand the negative impact the change is having on her community, and she knows she has to repair the damage.

Like many company leaders, Ellen is faced with the immense challenge of *Sustaining* her Free Agent community. These leaders are finding that even though the vision and infrastructure are in place, their communities require constant tending and nurturing. The Sustaining stage of our process is the time to commit to supporting and maintaining a fluid and dynamic Free Agent community. The purpose of this stage is to find ways to sustain individual allegiance to the corporate vision and goals. Sustaining requires constantly evaluating and enhancing existing systems and practices and developing new ones in response to emerging individual and community needs.

## The Sustaining Process

Sustaining a Free Agent community is an ongoing process because a community is a living organism that needs care and attention. It requires a firm commitment from senior management to invest in long-term solutions rather than quick fixes. Companies attempting to maintain a Free Agent community agree that the keys to success are committing to continuous change, keeping corporate systems aligned with corporate visions, asking for employee feedback, and expecting managers to assume new roles and responsibilities.

### *Committing to Continuous Change*

We find that many managers seem to believe that they will have to change only once; after that, everything will be taken care of forever. In companies committed to Sustaining a Free Agent community, managers understand that change is a continual process. They are entrusted with regularly identifying changes and adjustments that must be made to obtain the skills and results they need. When making decisions, they consider how to attain the most positive long-term environment for both Free Agents and their company.

Mike explains that shortly after he implemented significant changes, some of his managers seemed relieved. They thought that the changes were over and now things would return to normal. Mike patiently explained that in order for their company to remain competitive, they needed not only to build but also to maintain a community that could attract and retain value creators. The only "normal" they would ever again know was constant change.

### *Keeping Corporate Systems Aligned with Corporate Vision*

A major part of Sustaining is making sure that the organization's systems and practices remain aligned with the vision over time. New systems need to be congruent with the company's vision, and if they are not, they need to be realigned. Because Free Agents want expectations to be clear, inconsistencies between vision and practices negatively affect community and result in bad morale and lowered productivity.

### *Asking for Employee Feedback*

Free Agents want and need to provide input into Sustaining their community. They know whether their environment is enabling them to create their best work; if it is not, they usually can suggest changes. Some companies are using annual, and often quarterly, quality-of-life or employee-satisfaction surveys as one vehicle for obtaining this type of information from their Free Agents. Ellen, like many other managers, uses these surveys as a way to determine how her community is working. For these surveys to be useful, everyone in the organization needs to take them seriously, and management must use them as an impetus for change.

To be most valuable though, the survey questions need to reflect the issues that are the keys for both Sustaining community and adding to the company's financial value—issues such as clarity of purpose and methods of communication and control. In many companies, managers view these responses as a report card on how well they are meeting their Free Agents' needs. When areas for improvement are identified, managers know that they need to respond quickly to maintain credibility.

### *Expecting Managers to Assume New Roles and Responsibilities*

Managers are essential to Sustaining the Free Agent community. In the best of all worlds, all managers would be Free Agents themselves. But that is not a realistic expectation in most organizations, nor is it absolutely necessary. Many managers who have not fully committed to becoming Free Agents themselves are able to manage teams of Free Agents. The keys to their success are their ability to understand their Free Agents' needs and their willingness to assume new roles and responsibilities for meeting those needs.

Managers of Free Agents consider coaching their main responsibility and their primary obligation to their team and to their organization. As coaches they foster a safe environment that allows for resourcefulness, creativity, and risk taking. They facilitate change and learning (Boyett and Boyett, 1995, p. 185). When they are able to coach individuals to achieve their best, they are actively participating in Sustaining a culture of continuous improvement.

Because Free Agents are self-managing and are committed to doing their best work, the managers' primary focus is on providing their team members with:

- Clear direction and vision
- Responsibility, authority, and boundaries for decision making
- Respect for their expertise and skills
- Channels for two-way communication
- Recognition and reinforcement
- Tools for development and improvement

As competition increases, managers need to raise performance expectations constantly. For this reason, they have to implement a professional-development process for all their employees. This process identifies strengths and limitations, additional skills needed, development opportunities, and next steps within the company. Although going through this process is time consuming, managers see it as their principal strategy for enabling all employees to achieve their best. Megan, a manager in a large, internationally well-known company, explains that her organization restructures frequently. Every time employees move to a new position, they take their development plans with them and continue with a new manager. Managers realize the importance of providing continuity in development. Management sees this method as a good strategy for providing Free Agents with new opportunities to apply their skills in different areas while adding to their Portfolios of Assets. As Megan explains, "It's pretty crazy, but it seems to work for us."

## Sustaining a Dispersed Community

> Sustaining a community of Free Agents in the same building is difficult enough, but I have them all over the place. Some of my team members telecommute, and some are not even on our payroll. But they are all part of my team, and I believe that if they feel connected, they will produce the kind of results I need. It's my job to find a way to make them all feel like they belong.

Today's Free Agent marketplace adds some interesting challenges to the already complex problem of maintaining a cohesive corporate community. Companies have to hold together an increasingly dispersed workforce. They need to make everyone, regardless of that person's legal, financial, or physical relationship to the organization, feel like a valuable member of the community. This requirement is tricky, especially when you are dealing with remote workers, contingent workers, and outsourced workers. In order to maintain a highly productive and cohesive community, companies are feeling some urgency to find ways of integrating these individuals.

### *Remote Workers*

Jeff had been employed as a programmer with a financial institution for many years. When the daily, three-hour, round-trip commute became unbearable, Jeff negotiated a new arrangement with his employer. Because he provided an unusual and valuable combination of skills that the company wanted to retain, management agreed that he could work from an office in his home. He also had an office and shared an administrative assistant at his work location, and one day a week he was on-site. When working from his home office, he communicated via telephone, e-mail, and fax. His clients never suspected his change of venue, and he was more productive and motivated than ever. It was a win/win situation for everyone.

Jeff is one of a growing number of Free Agents who are employed by a company but work off-site, usually at home. This type of relationship provides flexibility for both sides. It enables individuals to control and manage their own time and production, while reducing operating costs for the organization.

In the past, most remote workers were in sales, but now they work in all areas and at all levels. Companies that used to negotiate informal agreements with individual remote workers are now implementing structured programs for entire groups and even departments. New technology has made this tremendous increase in the number of telecommuters possible. It is predicted that by 2002 a full 15 percent of the U.S. workforce will be telecommuting (LaPlante, 1995, p. 133).

As corporations are realizing the benefits of increased productivity coupled with reduced turnover and costs, they are becoming comfortable with this type of work relationship. Their two main areas of concern are how to manage output and how to make Free Agents feel like valuable members of the community. Free Agents are important team members with key skills, and they need to be granted independence and, at the same time, to be held accountable. Clear expectations, trust, and professional respect are the cornerstones that make this relationship work for both sides. Project leaders are forced to be clear about the parameters of the project and the expected outcome. Then they must trust the individuals to deliver. They need to identify check-in points and be on-call throughout the process.

Most of all, project leaders need to make these individuals feel like part of the team. Because remote workers do not interact in person, they can easily feel out of touch. Although some individuals do not mind, others crave community and teamwork (LaPlante, 1995, pp. 135–136). When working at home they miss the bonds and sense of community they had. Companies are using some of the following strategies to include their remote workforce:

- Providing adequate computer equipment, telecommunication hookups, and support services
- Including remote workers on the company's electronic network
- Encouraging them to come into the office weekly
- Scheduling monthly meetings for all employees
- Using videoconferencing when appropriate
- Including remote workers in making decisions that affect them, their projects, or their teams
- Notifying them immediately of decisions and changes
- Requiring progress reports and scheduling periodic feedback sessions
- Including remote workers in social events
- Providing managers and project leaders with the skills they need to develop trust and obtain results (LaPlante, 1995, p. 138)

Regardless of what else you do to include your remote Free Agents, face-to-face interaction is essential. On the days that Jeff is in the office, he can see everybody and catch up on news he has missed. Jeff, like many other remote workers, admits that the one thing he longs for is "just standing around shooting the breeze. It's not the same with e-mail." He misses the information he used to get when having a cup of coffee with colleagues or meeting them in the hall. He now realizes how much business is conducted that way and how much you lose when you are physically separated (LaPlante, 1995, p. 138).

The challenges associated with including remote workers are certainly not insurmountable, and overcoming them is well worth the effort. By permitting Free Agents to work off-site, companies are reducing their chances of losing good people. Jeff would have left the company if management had not allowed this new relationship. Many of his friends have left other companies that did not provide the flexibility they needed for their work and their personal lives. "I was one of the lucky ones. My manager thought it was a great idea and went to bat for me. It was actually a wise business decision. I am saving them money in many ways. Most of all, I am more productive than ever. Everyone benefits."

### *Professional Contingent Workers*

> Corporate demand for interim professionals and executives has created a whole new industry over the past few years. . . . As John Thompson, head of Imcor, states, "What's core today can be considered contingent tomorrow" [Fierman, 1994a, p. 33].

In 1994, *Fortune* noted that "one out of four of us is now a member of the contingent work force, people hired by companies to cope with unexpected or temporary challenges—part-timers, freelancers, subcontractors, and independent professionals" (Fierman, 1994a, p. 30).

Some of the contingent workforce is composed of Free Agents with professional skills who are hired for specific projects or distinct functions. This relationship satisfies the companies' need to obtain critical skills without the associated overhead and binding commitment. The legal profession provides an interesting example. The number of temporary lawyers increased from ten thousand in 1992 to more than forty thousand in 1995 (Sullivan, 1995, p. 44).

It is difficult to create ownership and community when your workforce is composed largely of contingent workers. In spite of reservations about confronting potential legal issues, sharing competitive secrets, and investing in training and development, companies that include their contingent workers as part of their ongoing community fare better than those that do not; they record increased productivity and improved outcomes (Fierman, 1994a, p. 34). These organizations develop a group of individuals with the skills they need and use them whenever possible. Workers identify with the company and feel that they are contributing to corporate goals. They become indoctrinated in the core values and principles of the company and understand how to get results quickly. When projects come along, they are up and running.

Ideally, these companies want their full-time employees to view these temporary workers as important additions to the community. To accomplish this goal and to be sure that temporary workers view themselves in the same way, some companies are implementing these relatively inexpensive but effective tactics:

- Sharing their corporate vision, goals, and directions with contingent workers
- Providing them with frequent feedback to acknowledge results and contributions and to identify areas for skill development
- Including them in office events, team photos, holiday parties, and newsletter articles
- Including them on the mailing list for company publications

- Asking them for suggestions about internal systems and management practices
- Inviting them to internal educational series
- Sharing the cost of attending professional or educational meetings with them
- Publicly or privately recognizing and rewarding their exceptional performance and accomplishments

### *Outsourced Workers*

As more and more companies are defining their vision and their missions, they are narrowing their permanent staff to the point where these workers deal with only the core of the business. Tasks that used to be performed internally are often subcontracted to outside individuals and companies in order to reduce costs. Some organizations are outsourcing entire departments such as customer service, public relations, payroll, and even human resources. In other large companies, functions such as mail distribution, administrative services, and finance are handled by employees on-site who are hired, paid, and managed by an external company. Some of these companies provide on-site managers to oversee their workers, monitor efficiency, and work with company managers (Klebnikov, 1995, p. 42).

For community building, these new relationships raise some interesting questions about inclusion, short-term commitment, and rewards. Legal precedent is still being set. When individuals with different employers are working side by side, how to align interests becomes an important question. With employees off-premises, as is often the case in customer service and fulfillment, these issues are not quite as prominent.

When Ellen realized that customer service was not part of the company's core and that someone else would probably be able to do it better and more cost effectively, she contracted with an outside company to staff and manage her company's customer-service center. Because the center was located in a different city, inclusion was not a problem. In order to provide seamless customer service, though, the individuals at the center needed to understand and believe in the company's purpose and vision. Ellen's company provided these employees with initial training, clear performance expectations, and procedural guidelines.

The tenets for Sustaining community with external Free Agents are the same as those that apply to internal, permanent staff. Aligning individual work with corporate vision and goals, providing individuals with the information and training they need, giving clear direction and feedback, recognizing and rewarding accomplishments, and including individuals in making decisions that affect them are actions that ensure quality and motivate individuals to achieve their best. By following these principles, managers create a community that meets corporate and individual needs. Some of these practices will work for you as you attempt to maintain a Free Agent community, and some will not. It is important to use these suggestions in the way that is best for your industry and your company. The next chapter describes three Free Agent communities in action.

*Chapter Twelve*

# Free Agent Communities in Action

> An organization acting as a community is a
> collective lifelong learner, responsive to change,
> receptive to challenge, and conscious of an
> increasingly complex array of alternatives.
> —K. Gozdz, *"Building Community as a Leadership Discipline"*

As we were reading and talking to people about Free Agent communities, we were struck by three models—entertainment, publishing, and high-tech—that seemed to us to embody the qualities and characteristics of those communities and that serve here as interesting illustrations. We are only observers of, not experts on, these communities; exceptions to our observations undoubtedly exist. Nevertheless, we want to share these ideas with you. For each model we present the background, an overview of the present situation, and a description of how it represents a Free Agent community.

Although these communities appear to be diverse, they have some similar features. All three are knowledge-intensive, employ individuals for their technical and creative expertise, create unique products, provide high compensation for value creators, and require flexibility, specialization, and intercompany cooperation and collaboration. Most important, internal and external factors have forced them to become Free Agent communities.

## Entertainment Model

The movie business is a good example of how an entire industry became a fluid Free Agent community. In the 1930s and 1940s movie making, as described in an article by Joel Kotkin and D. Friedman (1995), was a vertically integrated industry specializing in mass production. Seven major studios dominated production and controlled all the distribution channels. They employed predominantly permanent, highly skilled staff, located under one roof, who took care of all phases of production and distribution. All production was centralized and was contained in a specific geographic area known as Hollywood.

The grip that the large conglomerates had on all parts of the industry began loosening in the late 1940s and 1950s, creating an opening for new players. With the end of control over distribution and the entry of other competitive products, profit margins were driven down. Hollywood was forced to find ways of producing more creative and innovative films while reducing costs. The final blow was struck by television, which allowed people to view for free what they had been paying for.

Kotkin and Friedman explain that, in response, Hollywood was forced to reinvent itself long before other industries. As filmmaking became a craft instead of a commodity, all contributors—actors, writers, musicians, public-relations people, choreographers—had to combine the highest caliber of skills to produce a final product that could not be easily copied. This formula required that people specialize and excel at their crafts. As individuals became more capable though, they began demanding more pay. Soon the studios could not afford to keep them on staff.

Kotkin and Friedman note that as a result of this upheaval, a network industry has emerged consisting of entrepreneurs, specialists, and mostly small companies that work together on a project-by-project basis. A decrease in the number of large companies has opened the way for a virtual explosion of independent filmmakers, service providers, and related smaller companies.

As Kotkin and Friedman point out, flexibility, specialization, intercompany cooperation, and continuous learning characterize the Hollywood model today. Most of the work is performed by freelancers or small companies with fewer than ten employees. Learning a specialized craft and finding a way to fit it into the network economy is the key to success. Individuals and small companies find it especially important to form alliances, networks, and partnerships. Free Agents earn their reputation through their crafts. Their combined specialization and expertise result in the creation, production, and distribution of unique, high-quality products. The ability to offer the breadth of products and services needed to make this model work depends on independent Free Agents and the cooperation of those working in the many small and medium-sized firms.

In Hollywood the smartest thing to do with the competition is to join it. The high concentration of talent in the Los Angeles area constitutes an indispensable critical mass of resources available for any type of project. An expert team can be pulled together with incredible speed. To be chosen for those teams, Hollywood Free Agents and smaller companies must be learning continuously. Because of demanding clients and unceasing competition, technical virtuosity is critical to success. Constantly upgrading skills increases salability and desirability and is an individual's competitive edge. To meet client needs, work teams with specialized talents are constantly formed and then disbanded. Learning to deal with pressure and uncertainty is critical. Because projects tend to last from four to five months, to stay in the industry Free Agents must accept periods of unemployment. Flexibility in accepting a variety of projects ensures more consistent work. A producer tells us that "everyone works so hard to get the work. You have to always be proving yourself; you are only as good as your last project."

In this model, community is created around specialized crafts and the work itself. The intensity of the projects tends to create a strong sense of family and camaraderie. Criteria for selection on project teams are reputation, skill, credibility, and who you know—your network. Long-term alliances develop based on talent and skill and past working relationships. One director told us that he uses the same people over and over again. Smaller communities develop around single crafts. Craftspeople provide others in their community with support and up-to-date information about the industry and technology.

The Hollywood Free Agent community offers several advantages. The unusual concentration of talent allows for the quick acquisition of skilled people. The nature of the work lends itself to hiring the people best suited to projects on a short-term basis. And these people can quickly produce high-quality, innovative products that meet customers' stiff demands.

## Publishing Model

Publishing is an example of an industry that is in the throes of becoming a Free Agent community. As described in a Harvard Business School case study, the industry maintained a stable workforce composed primarily of highly skilled and educated knowledge workers through the mid-1980s. Individuals tended to spend their careers with one major company where they were offered opportunities for interesting projects and predictable advancements. However, since the mid-1980s the industry has experienced some major changes driven by declining operating margins, increasing pressure for profitability, changing customer demands, and the increasing complexity and sophistication of technology. Acquisitions became the prominent strategy for dealing with these forces, and the result was fewer major companies, greater segmentation, and an increase in niche presses. In order to be profitable, publishing houses had to pay attention to economies of scale and cost containment (Uyterhoeven, 1993, pp. 4–6).

The publishing industry today is much different than it was earlier. The industry is in the process of re-creating itself as a Free Agent community. With falling operating margins and increased competition, companies have become reluctant to maintain large in-house staffs. Instead they are maintaining a core set of functions within the company and using independent professionals for others. For example, historically, editing was the only contracted function. But aided by technology, companies now elect to accomplish as many other functions off-premise as possible, including reviewing and critiquing manuscripts, copyediting, proofreading, indexing, book and jacket design, pagination, warehousing, production, fulfillment, and publicity.

Some companies even employ external Free Agents as project managers. One publishing professional we interviewed commented, "It seems like everything happens somewhere else." In a well-known publishing company the only functions still performed internally are acquisitions, project management, marketing, editing, and finance and administration. For those who stay in-house, a lifetime career with one company is no longer the norm.

Because internal managers now have responsibility for managing an external workforce and implementing new ways of working, they need different skills. Along with freelancers and in-house employees, internal managers are reeling from the speedy introduction of new technology. One production manager explains that her biggest challenge is getting freelancers to learn the new systems so they do not hamper the entire project. Although she solves this problem by including both internal and external Free Agents in her training classes, other companies expect their freelancers to learn the technology on their own. Companies are developing and maintaining a cadre of freelancers who understand their business practices and goals and whom they use repeatedly.

In order to make this dispersed Free Agent community feel affiliated, managers confirmed they are using the variety of strategies we have already discussed, including

- Developing a clear vision that serves as a rallying point to keep everyone on track and to establish expectations
- Focusing on continuous learning by identifying areas for development and sometimes by providing training
- Recognizing external Free Agents with intangible rewards such as verbal recognition and reinforcement
- Developing two-way communication systems for feedback and evaluation

- Including external Free Agents in information sharing, decision making, and celebrations

Publishing is a Free Agent community in flux. At the present, it offers many opportunities for Free Agents who possess the necessary crafts and state-of-the-art technical skills. It provides companies with the flexibility and cost containment they are searching for. This is a community that is worth watching.

## High-Tech Model

In 1950 Santa Clara Valley, California, was the prune capital of the United States. The economy was primarily agricultural, with a handful of electronic and manufacturing businesses mixed in. Seven years later, a group of engineers founded Fairchild Semiconductor, which became the model for future start-ups and gave birth to what today is known as Silicon Valley (Cringely, 1992, pp. 37–38).

Many of the early high-tech entrepreneurs were mavericks in developing and applying technology, running their companies, and managing their people. Most of these companies were small operations that gave their employees the potential for huge future returns in exchange for total commitment. They were able to attract young, bright, creative people by offering exciting, groundbreaking work. They featured flat management structures and a high level of employee independence, which allowed freedom for innovation. By downplaying the traditional hierarchies, these companies were able to create environments that enabled talented people to flourish. Within a short time, Silicon Valley became internationally known for its concentration of youth, talent, innovation, risk taking, and success stories.

Corporate cultures throughout the Valley emphasized shared responsibility and common purpose. The energy generated became a powerful motivator. Stock options were a standard part of compensation plans for all employees instead of just for senior managers. Closed doors were replaced by cubicles; and people were encouraged to openly speak their minds. This new corporate attitude, combined with access to some of the country's finest universities, resulted in technological advances that have changed the world.

Silicon Valley attracts high-tech companies that are knowledge-and skill-driven, customer-focused, and open to change. The culture of the founding companies has carried over to today in the creation of environments that promote innovation. Companies continue to offer pioneering work and provide few hurdles to advancement for value creators.

High-tech companies in Silicon Valley have a tremendous need for skilled workers, and there are not enough individuals to meet this demand. This situation attracts young, mobile workers who are then granted a great deal of responsibility, authority, and autonomy; who work on important and challenging projects; and who have the possibility of amassing great wealth at an early age. It is not uncommon for thirty-year-olds to manage teams of fifty people.

Competition is stiff, and a sense of urgency dominates all businesses. The brass ring belongs to those companies that are ahead in technology and new-product development. Companies succeed by hiring the most highly skilled people, paying them well, and then pushing them to perform. Companies form alliances with universities and even competitors.

Because recruitment is extremely competitive, companies understand the importance of creating environments for attracting Free Agents. Catering to the most talented people is critical. Among the enticements that most companies offer are the following:

- Responsibility, power, and autonomy
- Extraordinary compensation, including stock options, signing bonuses and other incentives, sabbatical leaves, and special vacation trips

- Excellent benefits
- Constant learning opportunities
- Flextime so that employees can set their own hours
- Luxurious campuses, including gyms, basketball courts, and swimming pools
- Catered snacks and meals

But the demands are also enormous. The clock is ticking for everyone. Companies expect a great deal from Free Agents in terms of time and productivity. In most companies seventy-hour work weeks are normal. To survive, individuals must find and maintain a balance between their professional and personal lives, which is especially difficult in households with two Free Agents.

In return for the demands placed on them, people expect to be exposed to continual learning and development in short-term positions. From the beginning of their careers, individuals adopt a Free Agent mind set. Movement is rampant. No one expects to spend an entire career with one company. In fact, people manage their careers by moving from one company to another and building incredible Portfolios of Assets (Malone, 1995, p. 23).

Networking is critical for Free Agents who work in any of the industries in Silicon Valley. As in the entertainment and publishing models, Free Agents have large and active networks that provide them with easy and quick access to information and leads for projects and positions. To keep in touch with one another and to stay visible within their craft community, people attend conferences, workshops, and trade shows; communicate through e-mail; and belong to trade and professional associations.

The companies in Silicon Valley provide examples of ways to maintain a Free Agent community. They understand the importance of being perceived as good environments for Free Agents. By the nature of their work, they provide interesting and challenging projects. Many have clear visions that drive the organization and serve as a framework for their Free Agent community. They encourage and reward autonomy. They offer the possibility for extraordinary compensation, continuous learning, and professional development.

In return, the flourishing network of Free Agents must always add value to the organization. They need to keep their Portfolios of Assets current and be able to provide the market with the skills it needs now and in the future. They are expected to strive to perform well at all times and share responsibility for results. This successful alignment of individual needs with corporate goals produces a high-performing, highly productive, risk-taking Free Agent community.

The companies and people in these three communities are paving the way for others. The individuals working in them have experienced the challenges of becoming Free Agents and now enjoy the benefits. They accept the fact that they alone are responsible for their careers and future. They work hard at their professions and are continuously adding to their Portfolios of Assets. They know their worth in the marketplace and know what they can expect in return for their skills. They are the value creators that companies in any industry need and want for their continued success and growth. Out of necessity, many of the companies in these industries have also transformed themselves. In order to meet the changing needs and expectations of their customers and their Free Agent workforce, they realize the power and benefits of providing a place where Free Agents can come and work with others to produce their best results.

Other individuals and companies are joining these leaders as they begin to understand the realities of the new world of work, and they too are in the midst of change. Those who have already reclaimed their careers and transformed their workplaces know that the Free Agent model is the work world of the future.

# References


Ancona, D., and others. *Managing for the Future*. Cincinnati: South-Western, 1996.

Ashkenas, R., Ulrich, D., Jick, T., and Kerr, S. *The Boundaryless Organization*. San Francisco: Jossey-Bass, 1995.

Bellah, R. N., and others. *Habits of the Heart: Individualism and Commitment in American Life*. Berkeley: University of California Press, 1985.

Boyett, J. H., and Boyett, J. T. *Beyond Workplace 2000*. New York: NAL/Dutton, 1995.

Bridges, W. *Transitions: Making Life's Changes*. Reading, Mass.: Addison Wesley Longman, 1980.

Bridges, W. *JobShift: How to Prosper in a Workplace Without Jobs*. Reading, Mass.: Addison Wesley Longman, 1994.

Bristol-Myers Squibb Company. *Our Plan for Growth*. New York: Bristol-Myers Squibb Communications Department, 1996.

Case, J. *Open-Book Management: The Coming Business Revolution*. New York: HarperCollins, 1995.

Cassidy, J. "All Worked Up." *The New Yorker*, Apr. 22, 1996, pp. 51–55.

Collins, J. C., and Porras, J. I. *Built to Last: Successful Habits of Visionary Companies*. New York: HarperCollins, 1994.

Compaq Computer. "Compaq: Has IT Changed Your Life Yet?" *1995 Summary Annual Report*. Houston, Tex.: Compaq Computer Corporation, 1996.

Cringely, R. X. *Accidental Empires: How the Boys of Silicon Valley Make Their Millions, Battle Foreign Competition, and Still Can't Get a Date*. Reading, Mass.: Addison Wesley Longman, 1992.

Dent, H. S., Jr. *Job Shock*. New York: St. Martin's Press, 1995.

Drucker, P. F. *The Practice of Management*. New York: HarperCollins, 1954.

Drucker, P. F. "The Age of Social Transformation." *Atlantic Monthly*, 1994, *272*(5), 53–80.

Fierman, J. "The Contingency Work Force." *Fortune*, 1994a, *129*(2), 30–36.

Fierman, J. "The Perilous World of Fair Pay." *Fortune*, 1994b, *129*(12), 57–64.

Filipczak, B. "You're on Your Own: Training, Employability, and the New Employment Contract." *TRAINING*, Jan. 1995, pp. 29–36.

Gozdz, K. "Building Community as a Leadership Discipline." In M. Ray and A. Rinzler (eds.), *The New Paradigm in Business*. New York: Putnam, 1993.

Haas, R. "The Corporation Without Boundaries." In M. Ray and A. Rinzler (eds.), *The New Paradigm in Business*. New York: Putnam, 1993.

Hakim, C. S. "You Are Self-Employed." *National Business Employment Weekly*, May 15–21, 1994, pp. 13–14.

Handy, C. *The Age of Unreason*. Boston: Harvard Business School Press, 1989.

Handy, C. *Beyond Certainty*. Boston: Harvard Business School Press, 1996.

Heckscher, C. *White-Collar Blues*. New York: HarperCollins, 1995.

Hirsch, P. "Free Agents in a Takeover World." *GSB Chicago*, 1988, *11*(1), 16–19, 24.

Jacob, R. "The Struggle to Create an Organization for the Twenty-First Century." *Fortune*, 1995, *131*(6), 90–99.

Jaffe, D., Scott, C., and Tobe, G. *Rekindling Commitment*. San Francisco: Jossey-Bass, 1994.

James, G. "Industrial Age Management Becomes a Museum Piece." *Upside*, Feb. 1996, pp. 63–73.

Klebnikov, P. "Focus, Focus, Focus." *Forbes*, Sept. 11, 1995, pp. 42–44.

Kotkin, J., and Friedman, D. "Why Every Business Will Be Like Show Business." *Inc.*, Mar. 1995, pp. 64–78.

Kotter, J. P. "Leading Change: Why Transformation Efforts Fail." *Harvard Business Review*, 1995, *73*(2), 59–67.

LaPlante, A. "Telecommuting: Round Two." *Forbes ASAP*, Oct. 9, 1995, pp. 132–138.

Levine, D. "Companies Go On-Line but Avoid Tangling with the 'Net.'" *San Francisco Business Journal*, June 14–20, 1996, pp. 2A, 4A.

Malone, M. S. "Secrets of Job-Hopping from High-Tech Stars." *The New York Times*, Feb. 19, 1995, p. 23.

Markels, A., and Lublin, J. S. "Longevity—Reward Programs Get Short Shrift." *The Wall Street Journal*, Apr. 27, 1995, p. B1, B6.

Martin, J. B. "UCSF Change and the High Road to Excellence." *UCSF Magazine*, July 1996, p. 16, frontispiece.

Murray, M. "Thanks, Goodbye." *The Wall Street Journal*, May 4, 1995, pp. A1, A5.

Noble, B. P. "At Work: The Bottom Line on 'People' Issues." *The New York Times*, Feb. 16, 1995a, p. F23.

Noble, B. "If Loyalty Is Out, Then What's In?" *The New York Times*, Jan. 29, 1995b, p. B21.

O'Reilly, B. "The New Deal: What Companies and Employees Owe One Another." *Fortune*, 1994a, *129*(12), 44–52.

O'Reilly, B. "360-Degree Feedback Can Change Your Life." *Fortune*, 1994b, *130*(8), 93–131.

Ramirez, A. "AT&T Offer: One Said No, One Said Yes." *The New York Times*, Dec. 10, 1995, pp. C1, C11.

Richman, L. S. "Getting Past Economic Insecurity." *Fortune*, 1995, *131*(7), 160–164.

Runge, L. D. "The Manager and the Information Worker of the 1990s." *Information Strategy: The Executive's Journal*, 1994, *10*(4), 7–14.

Semler, R. *Maverick: The Success Story Behind the World's Most Unusual Workplace*. New York: Warner Books, 1993.

Serwer, A. E. "Layoffs Tail Off—But Only for Some." *Fortune*, 1995, *131*(5), 14.

Sherman, S. "A Brave New Darwinian Workplace." *Fortune*, 1993, *127*(12), 50–53.

Simons, R. "Control in an Age of Empowerment." *Harvard Business Review*, 1995, *73*(2), 80–88.

Stewart, T. A. "The Search for the Organization of Tomorrow." *Fortune*, 1992, *125*(10), 92–98.

Stewart, T. A. "How to Lead a Revolution." *Fortune*, 1994, *130*(11), 48–61.

Stewart, T. A. "Planning a Career in a World Without Managers." *Fortune*, 1995, *131*(5), 72–80.

Sullivan, R. L. "Lawyers a la Carte." *Forbes*, 1995, p. 44.

Tully, S. "Your Paycheck Gets Exciting." *Fortune*, 1993, *128*(11), 83–98.

Uchitelle, L. "The Rise of the Losing Class." *The New York Times*, Nov. 20, 1994, D1, D5.

Uchitelle, L., and Kleinfield, N. R. "On the Battlefields of Business, Millions of Casualties." *The New York Times*, Mar. 3, 1996, pp. A1, A14, A16–A17.

Uyterhoeven, H. "Harcourt Brace Jovanovich, Inc." Case Study 9–392–045, Harvard Business School, Sept. 10, 1993, pp. 1–36.

Waterman, R. H., Waterman, J. A., and Collard, B. A. "Toward a Career-Resilient Workforce." *Harvard Business Review*, 1994, *72*(4), 86–95.

Zemke, R. "The Call of Community." *TRAINING*, 1996, *33*(3), 24–30.

# For Further Information

Araoz, D. L., and Sutton, W. S. *Reengineering Yourself: A Blueprint for Personal Success in the New Corporate Culture*. Holbrook, Mass.: Bob Adams, 1994.

Boyett, J. H., and Conn, H. P. *Workplace 2000: The Revolution Reshaping American Business*. New York: NAL/Dutton, 1991.

Charland, W., Jr. *Career Shifting: Starting Over in a Changing Economy*. Holbrook, Mass.: Bob Adams, 1993.

Glassner, B. *Career Crash: America's New Crisis—and Who Survives*. New York: Simon & Schuster, 1994.

Hakim, C. S. *We Are All Self-Employed*. San Francisco: Berrett-Koehler, 1994.

Henton, D., and others. *Joint Venture's Index of Silicon Valley*. San Jose, Calif.: Joint Venture: Silicon Valley Network, 1995.

Hirsch, P. *Pack Your Own Parachute*. Reading, Mass.: Addison Wesley Longman, 1987.

Iansiti, M., and Stein, E. "Silicon Graphics, Inc." Case Study 9–695–06, Harvard Business School, Apr. 1995, pp. 1–22.

Johansen, R., and Swigart, R. *Upsizing the Individual in the Downsized Organization: Managing in the Wake of Reengineering, Globalization, and Overwhelming Technological Change*. Reading, Mass.: Addison Wesley Longman, 1994.

Kanter, R. M. *When Giants Learn to Dance*. New York: Simon & Schuster, 1989.

Kleinfeld, N. R. "The Company as Family, No More." *The New York Times*, Mar. 4, 1996, pp. A1, A8, A10.

Koonce, R. "Becoming Your Own Career Coach: Fourteen Winning Habits Can Get You from Where You Are to Where You Want to Be in Today's Workplace." *Training and Development*, Jan. 1995, pp. 18–25.

Pearce, J. A., II, and Robinson, R. B., Jr. *Strategic Management Formulation, Implementation, and Control*. Burr Ridge, Ill.: Irwin, 1994.

Pfeffer, J. *Competitive Advantage Through People*. New York: McGraw-Hill, 1994.

Rogers, E. M. *Silicon Valley Fever*. New York: Basic Books, 1994.

Schein, E. H. *Career Anchors: Discovering Your Real Values*. San Francisco: Pfeiffer, 1993.

Sher, B., with Gottlieb, A. *Wishcraft: How to Get What You Really Want*. New York: Ballantine Books, 1983.

Stack, J., with Burlingham, B. *The Great Game of Business*. New York: Doubleday, 1992.

Waitly, D. *Empires of the Mind*. New York: Morrow, 1995.

Waterman, R. H., Jr. *The Renewal Factor*. New York: Bantam Books, 1987.

# Index


A

Action plan, 44–45
*Age of Unreason, The* (Handy), 60
Ancona, D., 115, 119, 120, 132, 151
Ashkenas, R., 112, 114, 153
Asia, 59

B

Bacon, F., 50
Bellah, R. N., 86
*Beyond Workplace 2000* (Boyett and Boyett), 85
*Boundaryless Organization, The* (Ashkenas, Ulrich, Jick, and Kerr), 153
Boyett, J. H., 5–6, 85, 156
Boyett, J. T., 5–6, 85, 156
Bridges, W., 31, 34, 58, 66, 67
Bristol-Myers Squibb Company, 101
"Building Community as a Leadership Discipline" (Gozdz), 165
*Built to Last: Successful Habits of Successful Companies* (Collins and Porras), 99

C

Case, J., 104, 105, 115
Cassidy, J., 5
Changing workplace: anxiety of, 6–8; corporate challenge of, 12–14; independence in, 8–10; and loss of community, 6–7; and new ethic, 14–15; new skills in, 5; responding to, 1–15; and unwritten contract, 4–6
Collard, B. A., 3, 113, 127, 132
Collins, J. C., 99, 112
Communication, 103–105, 112–115
Community. *See* New community
Compaq Computer, 101
Compensation systems, 117–121
Contingent workers, 160–162
Continuous change, 154–155
Continuous learning, 132, 148
Control, 106–107
Corporate change: challenges of, 12–14, 91–93; and free agent needs and expectations, 86–90; need for, 85–89; and new community, 87–89; and process of building new community, 90–91
Corporate infrastructure: communication systems and, 112–115; compensation systems and, 117–121; performance-management systems and, 115–116; redefining of, 111–123; reward and recognition systems and, 121–123; and vision, 111–112
Corporate initiatives, 89
Corporate needs, 3, 126–128
Corporate positioning: benefits and, 134–135; developing opportunities and, 131–132; exit policy and, 133–134; hiring process and, 129–131; recruitment and, 128–131; and skill-based teams, 126–128. *See also* Positioning
Corporate separating: and clarity of purpose, 99–103; and developing a new vision, 95–101; and open communication, 103–105; and organizational control, 106–107; role of management in, 107–109. *See also* Separating
"Corporation Without Boundaries, The" (Haas), 1
Cringely, R. X., 170

D

Dent, H. S., Jr., 126
Development opportunities, 131–132
Dispersed community, 157–158
Downsizing, 5
Drucker, P. F., 86, 87, 105

E

Eastern Europe, 79
Entertainment community, 165–168. *See also* Free agent community
Evaluation, 148, 155
Exit policy, 133–134

F

Fairchild Semiconductor, 170
Fairness, perception of, 7
Fierman, J., 120, 160, 161
Filipczak, B., 65, 72
Financial constraints, 42–43, 76, 146
Flexibility, 144
*Fortune*, 160
Free agent: checklist for, 28–29; code of, 10–11; definition of, 3–4; needs and expectations of, 88–89; and new ethic, 14–15; relationship to workplace, 86. *See also* Free agent status
Free agent checklist, 151
Free agent community: and corporate positioning, 125–126; and corporate redefining, 111–112; and dispersed community, 157–163; entertainment model of, 165–168; high-tech model of, 170–173; maintaining of, 153–163; publishing model of, 168–170
Free agent process: challenges of, 26–28; and creating a new future, 19–21; feelings and, 23–25; four stages of, 21–22; positioning stage of, 63–82; redefining stage of, 49–61; separating stage of, 31–47; transition to, 25–26
Free agent status: anxiety and, 142–143; challenges of, 143–146; commitment to, 140–141, 154; priorities in, 145; strategies for, 146–150; sustaining of, 139–151
Friedman, D., 165–166

G

Gozdz, K., 87, 165

H

Haas, R., 1, 87, 92, 104
Hakim, C. S., 11
Handy, C., 9, 60
Harvard University, 131, 168
Hecksher, C., 6, 10, 13–14, 86–87
High-tech community, 170–173. *See also* Free agent community
Hiring. *See* Recruiting and hiring systems
Hirsch, P., 9–10
Hollywood, 166–168

I

*In the Age of the Smart Machine* (Zuboff), 131
Information sharing. *See* Communication
Ingrained beliefs, 33–34

J

Jacob, R., 112
Jaffe, D., 36, 107
James, G., 86, 93
Jick, T., 112, 114, 153
*JobShift: How to Prosper in a Workplace Without Jobs* (Bridges), 66

K

Kerr, S., 112, 114, 153
Klebnikov, P., 162
Kleinfield, N. R., 4–5, 6
Kotkin, J., 165–166
Kotter, J. P., 100, 101

L

LaPlante, A., 158, 159, 160
Levine, D., 114
Listening: in positioning, 70–71; in separating, 41
London Business School, 9
Lublin, J. S., 4

M

Malone, M. S., 172
"Manager and the Information Age, The" (Runge), 95
Manager responsibilities, 108–109, 156–157
Markels, A., 4
Market fit, 78, 126
Marketability, 142, 144
Markets. *See* Positioning

Martin, J. B., 111
Micromanaging, 107
Middle East, 77
Murray, M., 5, 7

## N

Networks, building and maintaining, 73–74, 149–150
New behaviors, 23–25
New community: building of, 90–91; and corporate change, 87–90; models of, 165–173
*New ethic*, 14–15
*New York Times*, 4
Noble, B. P., 4

## O

*Open-Book Management: The Coming Business Revolution* (Case), 104
O'Reilly, B., 7, 8, 116
Outsourced workers, 162–163
Ownership, sense of, 38

## P

Peace Corps, 79
Performance-management systems, 115–116
Porras, J. I., 99, 112
Portfolio of assets: assembly of, 54–61; continued redefinition of, 22; desires and, 58; exploring markets for, 64–82, and free agent process, 21–23; personal characteristics and, 57–58; preferred working environment and conditions, 59; professional development of, 60; professional goals and, 58–59; and redefining, 50; skills for, 56–57; special knowledge and expertise, 57; values for, 55–56
Positioning: and markets, 65–67; persistence in, 77–78; and selection of market, 78–79; and selling portfolio of assets, 79–82; skills in, 69–72; strategies for, 72–78; stresses of, 67–69. *See also* Corporate positioning
Procter & Gamble, 5
Professional career guidance, 43, 53
Professional goals, 58
Project work, 76, 147
Publishing community, 168–170. *See also* Free agent community

## R

Ramirez, A., 3
Recognition. *See* Reward and recognition systems
Recruiting and hiring systems, 128–131
Redefining: and assembly of portfolio of assets, 54–61; and desires, 58; obstacles to, 50–52; and personal characteristics, 57–58; and preferred working conditions, 59; and professional goals, 58–59; skills for, 56–57; special knowledge and expertise and, 57; strategies for, 52–54; and values, 55–56. *See also* Corporate infrastructure
Reframing beliefs, 41–42
Relationship to workplace: concept of, 32–34; of employee, 3; of free agent, 86
Remote workers, 158–160
Research, 70
Reward and recognition systems, 121–123
Runge, L. D., 95, 106

## S

Santa Clara Valley (California), 170
Saudi Arabia, 77
Scott, C., 36, 107
Security, 4, 6, 50, 88, 142–143
Self-defeating behavior, 35–40
Semler, R., 103
Separating: as attitude transition, 31–34; denial and, 36–37; as emotional transition, 33–34; and fear, 37–38; kinds of endings and, 34–35; and moving on, 45–47; pain of, 35–36; and self-defeating behavior, 38–40; skills for, 40–42; strategies for, 42–45. *See also* Corporate separating
Serwer, A. E., 4
Sherman, S., 91–92
Silicon Valley (California), 80, 170, 171, 172
Simons, R., 107
Skills, 56, 60, 69, 126–128
Special knowledge and expertise, 37
Stewart, T. A., 107, 131

Sullivan, R. L., 161
Sustaining process: and diverse community, 157–163; of free agent community, 154– 157; of free agent status, 139–151

## T

Telecommuting. *See* Remote workers
Tobe, G., 36, 107
Traditional ways of thinking, 40–42
Tully, S., 118, 120

## U

Uchitelle, L, 4–5, 6, 32
"UCSF Change and the High Road to Excellence" (Martin), 111
Ulrich, D., 112, 114, 153
University of Chicago Graduate School of Business, 9
University of Michigan, 91–92
Unwritten employer-employee contract, 4–5, 6
Uyterhoeven, H., 168

## V

Vision statements: and corporate separating, 100–102; examples of, 101; uses of, 103

## W

Waterman, J. A., 3, 113, 126, 132
Waterman, R. H., 3, 113, 126, 132
Work environment, 1–15, 59, 86, 96
World War II, 4, 32

## Z

Zemke, R., 7, 9, 14, 86
Zuboff, S., 131

from Runge, L. D. "The Manager and the Information Worker of the 1990s." *Information Strategy: The Executive's Journal*, 1994, *10*(4), 7–14. Copyright © 1994 by Research Institute of American Group. Used with permission.

Chapter Eight: epigraph reprinted from Martin, Joseph B. "Markets and Miracles." *UCSF Magazine*, July 1996, frontispiece. Extract on page 112: Jacob, R. "The Struggle to Create an Organization for the Twenty-First Century." *Fortune*, 1995, *131*(6), 90–99. Copyright © 1995 by Time, Inc. All rights reserved.

Chapter Eleven: epigraph reprinted from Ashkenas, R., Ulrich, D., Jick, T., and Kerr, S. *The Boundaryless Organization*. San Francisco: Jossey-Bass, 1995, p. 63. Extract on page 160: Fierman, J., "The Contingency Work Force," *Fortune*, 1994, *129*(2), 30–36. Copyright © 1994 by Time, Inc. All rights reserved.

Chapter Twelve: epigraph reprinted from Gozdz, K. "Building Community as a Leadership Discipline." In *The New Paradigm in Business*. New York: Putnam, 1993, p. 108.